# The Microsoft® Crabby Office Lady Tells It Like It Is: Secrets to Surviving Office Life

*Annik Stahl*

PUBLISHED BY
Microsoft Press
A Division of Microsoft Corporation
One Microsoft Way
Redmond, Washington 98052-6399

Copyright © 2006 by Microsoft Corporation

Library of Congress Control Number 2006924465
978-0-7356-2272-2
0-7356-2272-8

Printed and bound in the United States of America.

1 2 3 4 5 6 7 8 9    QWE    1 0 9 8 7 6

Distributed in Canada by H.B. Fenn and Company Ltd.

A CIP catalogue record for this book is available from the British Library.

Microsoft Press books are available through booksellers and distributors worldwide. For further information about international editions, contact your local Microsoft Corporation office or contact Microsoft Press International directly at fax (425) 936-7329. Visit our Web site at www.microsoft.com/mspress. Send comments to mspinput@microsoft.com.

Microsoft, ClearType, Encarta, Entourage, Excel, FrontPage, Hotmail, InfoPath, Internet Explorer, JScript, MSN, OneNote, Outlook, PowerPoint, Segoe, SharePoint, Verdana, Visio, and Windows are either registered trademarks or trademarks of Microsoft Corporation in the United States and/or other countries. Other product and company names mentioned herein may be the trademarks of their respective owners.

The example companies, organizations, products, domain names, e-mail addresses, logos, people, places, and events depicted herein are fictitious. No association with any real company, organization, product, domain name, e-mail address, logo, person, place, or event is intended or should be inferred.

This book expresses the author's views and opinions. The information contained in this book is provided without any express, statutory, or implied warranties. Neither the authors, Microsoft Corporation, nor its resellers, or distributors will be held liable for any damages caused or alleged to be caused either directly or indirectly by this book.

**Acquisitions Editor:** Juliana Aldous
**Project Editor:** Kathleen Atkins
**Production Services and Editing:** Steve Sagman, Studioserv
**Copy Editor:** Jennifer Harris

Body Part No. X12-21112

*For Catherine Emily Figg Dart: Eternal best friend, relentless believer.*
*And for my lovely daughter, Bian, who is (almost) never the Crabby Office Baby.*

# Contents at a Glance

# Table of Contents

# Acknowledgments

There are so many people in my life—both my professional life and my personal life (often overlapping)—whom I must acknowledge and thank. Some of these people worked on this book with me; some of them have been a part of the Crabby Office Lady column since its inception; some hopped on board a bit later to help keep the column going strong; and some have been loyal readers of the Crabby columns—whether or not they liked them, understood them, or even wanted to read them in the first place. (Now that's true love.)

And so, my grateful recognition goes out to:

- My parents, Stanley and Yvonne Stahl, whose love for and belief in me, both as a mother and as a writer, enabled me to summon the energy to write this book. (And let's not forget the many adventures in babysitting and meal preparing that gave me those indispensable breaks when I really needed them.)

- My beautiful, bright, and (almost) never crabby 4-year-old daughter, Bian Baruch Stahl, to whom this book is dedicated, and who sometimes worked side-by-side with me after dinner on her own imaginary "computer," writing her own book. (Shel Silverstein and Marc Brown may have a competitor.)

- My sister and brother-in-law, Erika and Dave Kaye, for their encouragement and support throughout it all (and whose rah-rah attitude emboldened me to believe in my work and myself).

- My brother, Steve Stahl, whose never-ending jokes about the "Crappy Office Lady" enabled me take myself a bit less seriously.

- Marcie Munishor and her family, for all their love, acknowledgment of my hard work, and confidence in the work I do (not to mention who I am).

- My best friend of many lifetimes, Catherine Dart, to whom this book is also dedicated. Lerve, luff, loave, Sistah.

- My not-so-computer-literate friends (and you know who you are) who've read (and reread) the Crabby Office Lady columns (whether or not you've wanted to).

- Steve Sagman and Jennifer Harris, project manager, tech reviewer, editor, copy editor, and layout artist (five titles, two people—you do the math), who made my writing better and clearer than it could ever have been on its own. Late nights, early mornings—we spent them together...virtually.

- Kathleen Atkins, project editor, whose positive feedback, optimism, and advice kept me moving forward during the writing of this book.

- Juliana Aldous, Microsoft Learning program manager, whose work helped make my book dreams come true.

- Jim St. George, the talented artist who created the original Crabby Office Lady logo, and who worked tirelessly with me back in 2002 on getting her *just right* (lipstick mark on the coffee cup and all).

- Patricia Bradbury, book cover designer, and Jessie Good, chapter opener artist, both of whose work truly captured the spirit of Crabby.

- Kevin Grace, a Crabby Office Lady column editor, wordsmith, and friend, whose sense of humor often exceeds my own.

- Jean Philippe Bagel, possibly the nicest Frenchman I know. *Merci, bon ami; J'apprécie ton support et ton amitié.*

- Janet Galore, Jeff Olund, and Shelley Benson, managers at Microsoft who've believed enough in the power and influence of Crabby to continue taking the gamble to help keep her alive and moving forward.

- Michael Bolinger, the current Crabby Office Lady editor, whose gentle editing style and sharp sense of humor helped me keep the columns fresh...even while I was writing this book.

- The folks on the Microsoft Learning team who worked on this project—a big bunch of people who understood my idea of this book...and then helped make it happen.

- And last, but definitely not least, the *entire* Office Assistance and Worldwide Services Team, composed of writers, editors, copy editors, designers, site managers, content specialists, testers, internal tools teams, program managers, managers, administrative assistants, and developers (take a breath), without whose tireless dedication to making the Office programs understandable and useful my work would be impossible. A simple acknowledgment can't express how thankful I am to all of you for your zeal and commitment to making sure our customers (and my readers) understand the sometimes-complicated tools at their disposal.

# Introduction to the Crabby Office Lady

*The community stagnates without the impulse of the individual. The impulse dies away without the sympathy of the community.*

— *William James*

I normally write a weekly column, and now I've written a book. It's been a very different experience, and one that I've really enjoyed. (Well, mostly—those late nights with a wakeful toddler in the house can truly test one's stamina and enterprise.) But writing a book made me really consider and ponder who the Crabby Office Lady is, what her reach is (and could be), and whether what led to her online success could also be a guiding force for success in print. Would the regular Crabby Office Lady column readers want to shell out their hard-earned cash for a book instead of just reading the free, online weekly column? Ah, there's the rub... I figured I'd just have to see about that, and I was willing to put in the work and take that chance. And lucky for me (very, very lucky for me), so were my publishers.

After I wrote my proposed outline for the publishers, I realized that I had a lot more to say, and that there was much more I *could* say in a book than I had room for in an online column. And so, here I am. (And here you are. It's a pleasure to meet you, and thanks for coming.)

In 2005, the Crabby Office Lady column had more than 6 million readers (and viewers of her videos). While this is a good selling point for an online column, books and Internet content don't match up. It's my hope—and my belief—that you will see the value of having a printed Crabby Office Lady book in your library. I'm a voracious reader myself—fiction, nonfiction, book reviews, magazines, newspapers, personal essays, poetry, whatever—and I do think that this book is something completely different from anything that is already out there. (Hey, my mom says so, too, and I'm sure you know that she is completely objective...)

# How the Crabby Office Lady Came to Be

In late 2001, the Crabby Office Lady was born. Not born in the usual way (although in today's world, *usual* is a somewhat fluid term), but she *was* born. Crabby (as she is affectionately known) was born from an idea, from a brainstorm, and from a necessity. (As Plato said, "Necessity is the mother of invention.")

## Microsoft Office Online: A Bit of History

In 2001 and 2002, the Microsoft Office Online Web site was in transition. At that time, the site was called Microsoft Office Tools on the Web, and like today's Office Online Web site, this site offered assistance articles, templates, downloads, and clip art. What was missing—although we at Microsoft Office didn't exactly know it at the time—was content that *showed* people how to accomplish simple or complicated tasks (online training and demos); the ability to tell Microsoft what worked and what didn't work for you (the option to rate the site's content and give feedback about it); and something that talked to and helped customers in a real way, in real language, written by real people with some of the same problems that you were having (bring in the regular columnists).

That's where I—meaning the Crabby Office Lady—came in.

In 2001, the Office Tools on the Web site consisted of a big team of people (of which I was a member). We wrote the articles, created the templates, and programmed the site (meaning that we decided what types of content would go on the site where, when, and in what order). So we began having many, many meetings where we discussed the necessity of making sure that the Web site was as current as the products it was representing. We looked at magazines (online and in print), newspapers (again, online and in print), and at our competitors' Web sites, and we also took a hard look at our own site. What we came away with was this:

- We wanted to create a site where Office customers (and customers-to-be) could go and feel like they were a part of a community of other people using the same tools.

- We wanted a site that showed that we understood our customers' issues—and a site that struggled mightily to solve those issues.

- We wanted a site that was valuable enough to become the all-encompassing, one-stop assistance-shopping site for Office customers.

In other words, some big changes had to happen. And I was part of the team assigned to make that change happen.

## Crabby Office Lady: A Bit of History

In the winter of 2001, I was taking some time off my work as an assistance article writer and template creator for Microsoft Office. At that time, my daughter was still not born; therefore, I had some leisure time in my rainy Seattle home to sit with a glass of wine by the fire with my dog, Ry (yes, named after the musician Ry Cooder). And that is when the "Aha!" moment happened.

In a very short time, I came up with the idea of becoming a regular columnist writing for the then-current Office Tools on the Web site. My vision was this: create a character who would be an ongoing presence on the Web site (whatever this site was going to morph into), someone whose columns garnered an audience that came to enjoy, rely on, and even bookmark them as a Favorite in their browser. I had this vision, really, to create a sort of a funny (yet helpful) Dave Barry, a pedantic (yet humorous) William Safire, a self-help (yet somewhat grumpy) Dear Abby. What I was sure I *didn't* want was a typical Microsoft employee to be the name on the byline. I wanted to *humanize* Office.

**Note** To be honest, I already knew that the general public didn't really think of Microsoft as an "everyperson" sort of company, a company that used humor to get the point—any point—across. Hey, I've seen the TV commercials and print ads; I've read the scathing reviews. I don't live in a vacuum. *Funny* is not the first word that comes to mind when you think of Microsoft. You think I don't know that?

And so, I began to imagine someone who could represent the Office-using public—someone who understood the issues and troubles that regular people faced and struggled with during their daily lives in the office (and with Office). And that is how Crabby came into the world.

In 2003, the good-old Office Tools on the Web site retired (and is, I believe, still living the high life in a nicely appointed retirement community in Palm Desert). That's when I really began to work on my vision of who Crabby could be. And really, not much has changed since that initial "Aha!" moment. I still see Crabby as the old-timey secretary or administrative assistant: someone who is the first person you see when you walk through the door of a company's offices, be it a large or small company. Her desk is littered with half-filled foam cups of coffee (encircled with lipstick marks—a different color for every day of the week, of course). Her morning greeting may be grumpy—she is quick to give you the disapproving glance over her reading glasses if you've breached office protocol (such as tardiness or a dress-code violation), and while she may not greet you in the morning the way your granny might, she knows everything about you, nonetheless. Crabby knows your spouse's or partner's name (and birthday), your kids' names (and birthdays), your pets' names (and birthdays, not to mention Fido's and Fifi's personal ailments). Crabby knows how to get you the best table at the hottest restaurant in town when your in-laws are in town, and she is also an expert plumber and is not afraid to get her hands wet (or dirty).

But perhaps more importantly, Crabby knows, for instance, how to reformat your hard drive while saving your previous settings and precious documents, how to install only the Office features you want, how to import financial data from the Web, and when to use Microsoft Word and when to, once and for all, dive into Microsoft OneNote. She knows what constitutes "spam" and what is real, true information—tips that are necessary for your work, for the health of your computer, and for your company. Crabby can also help you plan your vacation, giving you tips about the best airfare and car rental deals on the Net, and can give you advice so that you don't return to an overstuffed Inbox and an underappreciated assistant.

Moreover, Crabby knows where the bodies are buried (not to mention the paperclips and sticky notes). In other words, I began to see—and still see—Crabby as an indispensable part of every office. She is a swivel-chair guru, a woman with a hard edge and a soft heart.

However, in the 5 years that I've been writing this column, I have not *pleased* all of my customers all of the time. I have *assisted* a good many of them part of the time, made some of them *laugh* another part of the time, and either *shocked* or *angered* a few of them more than one at a time. (So I figure I have all bases covered. Even the angry ones are paying attention.)

Some people thought that the Crabby caricature was misogynistic; some thought her face was too ethnic (while some thought not enough); and some thought there were enough crabby people in the workplace and that they didn't need to take the advice of a made-up one. (One woman even wrote to ask me why we didn't create a "sexist beat-you-down Crabby Office Man." I wrote back and told her that he had been fired...and that I had taken over his corner office.) But these people were in the minority.

When I wrote the first column, I set up an e-mail address so that people could actually write to me and tell me what they thought. This was prescient of me; after publishing the first column, I received more than 500 letters that week—90 percent of which were positive and expressed an excitement about having a "real" person who seemed to understand their daily work issues. And it's good that people took the time to write, because I can tell you that management—not to mention the Microsoft legal team—blanched when they read the first column. They weren't used to seeing their employees actually talk to their customers in a manner, well, in the manner in which Crabby speaks and writes. I call this "real talk," and apparently there was a need for it.

For one year, I wrote the column once a month, while continuing to do my regular job (writing assistance articles, creating templates, and programming the Web site). Because of Crabby's success and the demand for more columns, the next year, I wrote the column twice a month. In 2003, I began to write the column on a weekly basis and it became my full-time job. Since I started writing the column in 2002, I have had four managers, three editors, and more copy editors than I can even remember. All of these people have helped make the Crabby Office Lady columns a success, and I am grateful to them. It takes a village to raise a child...and it takes a big team to keep a column alive and well.

## Why You Need the Crabby Office Lady

While the Crabby Office Lady is represented as a caricature, I am, of course, a real person. I am not—nor have I ever been—a team of writers, a marketing mouthpiece, or—what I believe the general public thinks the majority of Microsoft employees are—a 25-year-old, naturally technically inclined, male Microsoft employee (in this case, posing as a middle-aged woman). Let's get this straight: I am also not a crabby middle-aged woman with cat-eye glasses and a swept-up hairdo who has been married (and divorced) three times. I'm a passionate, *almost*-middle aged woman *posing* as a cantan-kerous—yet helpful and humorous—middle-aged woman. I'm loud, I'm honest, and I'm happy to represent Microsoft...in a way that is, well, a bit unusual for a high-tech company. And yes, there is a bit of the Crabby Office Lady in me (or I wouldn't be able to write in the style I do).

OK, so I've been creative—what's in it for you? Well, let's start with me.

For me, Crabby provides a certain amount of job security (and a fun, *really* fun job, at that), as well as a real way to connect with real people. As for you? You get tips and tricks for how to make the most of Office products, and you also get someone who understands what it's like to spend all day every day in a workplace, one that may or may not be situated in your dream location. You get a break from the regular help topics and assistance articles (that are useful when you need immediate assistance). You get real-world scenarios, useful ideas, and perhaps, if I've done my job, a chuckle here and there.

## What Is in This Book

This book's title says it all. It's about surviving life in the office. It's about dealing with difficult people when you need to collaborate with them; it's about understanding what all those computing terms mean; it covers getting a handle on your e-mailing tasks (and manners); and it's about how to prepare to go on vacation and not have all that post-trip bliss washed away your first hour back.

I don't believe that being helpful and being humorous are mutually exclusive. I also don't believe that you can—or even should—separate your work-self from your home-self. Donning circulation-constricting garments like pantyhose and ties (while these items are rare on the main Microsoft campus, I know that they exist) doesn't—or at least shouldn't—stop the blood flow to your funny bone. (If it does, go up a size.)

What I'm trying to say is, if you enjoy editorial cartoons and funny pages along with your front-page headlines, the Crabby Office Lady is your gal. If it's all business today, and you just want straight news without the sharp insights and clever asides (well, some people don't want these things, you know), you'll find help topics and other types of Microsoft Office Online content that will take care of you.

This book is about how to survive—and thrive—in the office using Microsoft Office, one of the (if not *the*) most widely used software products in the business sector. I try to do all this with real-life examples, with humor, and with natural language. I don't really get a lot from books that use terms that I have to constantly look up in the computer dictionary, and I didn't want to write a book that made my readers have to do that either.

# What Is Not in This Book

This is not a "how-to" book. There are many of those types of books out there written by people much smarter and more eloquent at deciphering code and documenting procedures than I am. While I may offer a procedure or two to get my point across, my goal, for this book, is to give you the bigger picture about how to make the most of your time while you're at work. And while I do work for Microsoft and my specialty is Microsoft Office products, this book goes above and beyond just Word, Excel, PowerPoint, Outlook, and the other Office programs that you use every day. For example, I will not walk you through how to set up rules in Outlook, how to transpose Excel columns to rows, or even how to insert video into your PowerPoint presentations. What I will do is tell you when and why to do that stuff and then give you links to more information that *will* walk you through those processes.

# Who This Book Is For

When I was approached about a Crabby Office Lady book, one of the biggest challenges was to figure out whom the audience would be—who was going to read this book? I came up with any different scenarios regarding who might want to have this book on hand:

**Managers welcoming a new employee on the job**    This book is helpful and yet entertaining (or should be, anyway); it gives insight into office life as well as links to how to get help with the tools used in most offices: Microsoft Office programs.

**Your mom and dad**   You've finally gotten your folks (or grandfolks) online—they're sending e-mail messages, attaching photos of their zinnias, and (God love 'em) passing off every joke, rumor, and chain letter that comes their way. This book is a gentle way of introducing them to the basic rules and regulations of e-mail, to computer terms, and to setting up their Office programs so that they're not starting their computing life with frustration and aggravation (and calling you every 15 minutes to solve their problems).

**You**   Everyone needs a break during the daily humdrum of life in the office, and one more visit to the kitchen for some really old coffee is just not doing it for you. And going online to look at sports scores or the stock market's performance or to do a little online shopping might be against company policy (not to mention visiting Web sites that you have no business visiting while at work...or possibly ever). I hope that this book can give you a laugh or two and ease some of your boredom, while at the same time teaching you some tips and tricks about how to use Microsoft Office and make the most of your daily work.

So...welcome. I hope you enjoy reading this book as much as I enjoyed writing it. It just may be the first technical book that you read from start to finish... (I can't promise there won't be a quiz at the end of it, bright-eyes, so keep one of those eyes on the prize.)

Chapter One

# Stand Up Straight and Mind Your E-Mail Manners

*Good manners are made up of petty sacrifices.*

— *Ralph Waldo Emerson*

Everyone talks about it, everyone uses it, and everyone, at some time, has complained about it. Electronic mail (you know it as *e-mail*) has become the standard for how companies communicate with employees, how employees communicate with each other, how consumers communicate with companies, how moms and dads keep track of kids, how kids keep track of their friends, and even how teachers reach out to students (even when students have no desire to be reached out to). In other words, nearly all of us are digitally connected, accept it or not.

# E-Mail as the Modern Method of Communication

It's hard to pinpoint when e-mail became just another part of our culture—both at work and at home. But it really doesn't matter, because it's here, and it's here to stay (until telepathy becomes a bit more standard, and then heaven help the one whose job it is to deal with the spelling and grammar—not to mention *morality*—checker). Computers can do it, cell phones can do it, and all sorts of wireless devices can do it. And maybe, in the not-so-distant future, we'll be able to use a combination of special glasses combined with eye blinks and nose twitches to send and receive e-mail. It's easy, it's quick, and it's—usually, supposedly, in the best of all possible worlds—painless.

But like any form of communication, e-mail has positive and negative sides. It has good and bad points. It has yin, it has yang; it is both the good twin and the evil twin. And you, the human being creating and sending this e-mail, also embody those qualities. Sure, e-mail is a great way to pop off a little note to your best friend when you don't have time for a full-blown typed (or, heaven forbid, handwritten) letter. And when it comes to keeping in touch with far-off relatives (whom you'd like to call more often but whose time zones you can never keep straight), e-mail can't be beat. For us working stiffs, using e-mail to track the status of a project and all those involved in it is ideal, not to mention the most efficient method of communication, if done right. Yes, e-mail has its place, and an elevated place it has become. Your boss sends it, and your mom sends it, your granny and your six-year-old have found a way to communicate with each other on a daily basis with it. And you, of course, start and end the day with it.

But we can abuse (and be abused by) e-mail, and yes, it can be painful. Frankly, all of us have felt the uncomfortable sting of bad e-mail etiquette. In fact, this inevitable Inbox cramping can take many shapes, and like any sort of pain, it can happen any time of day or night, in any time zone, and to people of all ages, shapes, colors, and levels of technological prowess.

However, all is not lost. I'm here to ease everyone's pain by helping you recognize

- What constitutes bad e-mail
- How you can avoid being (prepare yourself for this hackneyed, hip term) an *enabler* of bad e-mail and the people who send it
- When to send e-mail and when to get off your duff and step down the hall, walk down the street, or get on the phone instead of hiding behind your keyboard

But am I being completely selfless in my motivation? I am not. By teaching you a bit about what constitutes bad e-mail manners and how to avoid the pitfalls that lead to such behavior, I'm sparing myself some daily digital unpleasantness. In other words, altruism is not my purpose (at least not completely).

I have decided to start this book by launching into one of the most pressing, unsettling, and uncomfortable issues in the life of a typical office worker: e-mail etiquette. No matter how much e-mail you send or receive, you've been touched—no, *harassed*—by the bad manners of others (or, I'm sorry to say, of yourself).

As I mentioned earlier, e-mail has become the communication form of first resort, particularly at work, and people, I'm here to tell you that you have gotten sloppy. Have you forgotten one of the basic and crucial tenets of office life (not to mention life in general)? It's "treat others as you would like to be treated." For the purpose of our discussion, I couldn't care less whether you believe that because I'm a working woman with a working arm (not to mention stiletto heels that could dice a ripe tomato in your bare hand), you don't need to hold the door open for me. And if you don't want to put your napkin on your lap, that's your lap's business. In that same vein, if you feel the need to call my house after 10 P.M., you go right ahead. (I just won't be answering— you'll hear my clever outgoing message instead.)

But when it comes to your e-mail manners, well, you and I need to have a sit-down. (And if Tony Soprano were available, I'd invite him, too.) Because I'm getting a lot of mail from you that is, well, let's just say, less than professional and with more *attitude* than I need to be reading. (And you wonder why I call myself *crabby*?) Crabby readers, we need to talk basics; we need to remember that it's people we're sending e-mail to, not computer servers. And I'm here to shout out to you that it's never too late to rethink how you're using this standard, modern, and prevalent form of communication. Read on and then become a role model for others. Make me proud, won't you?

# Crabby's Top 10 E-Mail Crabs

It's true that I have a few complaints when it comes to e-mail. But please don't get me wrong. It's not that I don't like to hear from you; I just have this deep desire for everyone with an e-mail account to get on board with some basic and (the word my father likes to use) *civilized* rules and regulations when it comes to communicating in this fashion. Hence, my top 10 e-mail crabs.

So before I jump into the part of this book that will, I hope, help you to manage your daily dose of all kinds of e-mail, I want to give you, straight off the bat, some of the reasons why the topic of e-mail etiquette is so near and dear to my heart. Let's jump right into the things that irritate me (and if I'm in tune with my readers, irritate you, too).

## Crab #1: Discretion Is the Greater Part of Replying

Imagine that you've received a piece of company-wide e-mail from someone in your very large organization. If you have the impulse, the hard-to-control urge, to respond, rest assured that every member of your very large organization does not want to have to read your personal feelings about that message, no matter how witty or urbane you might think your response is. This may be a hard fact to swallow, but it's true. What I'm saying here is twofold:

1.  Really consider, really think hard, whether you need to reply *at all*. Replies like "Me too!" or "I'll be there!" are quite unnecessary and waste not only your time but also the time of the people reading them.

    For example, if I get an e-mail from my boss, Bill Gates, inviting me to the annual company picnic, I'm fairly certain that he doesn't need to know if I'll be attending with one child or eight. Not that he doesn't care, mind you—in fact, Bill is well known as one of the great philanthropists of our time. It's just my personal opinion that Bill probably has other e-mail messages that may be more pressing than my personal response about the annual summer outing—shocking but true.

    This takes me to the next fact...

2.  If you do need to reply to the sender, please, reply *only* to the sender; there is no need to click the **Reply All** button. Consider the dozens, hundreds, or even hundreds of thousands of recipients who will be privy to your thoughts and opinions. Your reply might be considered spam. You may be thought of as careless or even silly.

So if you really believe that you have something to say to everyone on the **To** and the **Cc** lines, well, think very hard about that. And then think again. Learn the difference between **Reply** and **Reply All**.

# Crab #2: STOP YELLING AT ME

USING ALL CAPITAL LETTERS IS NOT ONLY RUDE AND IRRITATING, IT'S ALSO HARD TO READ. (And doesn't it make you lean your head back, to stave off the visual assault?) Save your caps for special occasions, such as those times when you want your recipient to know you're shouting. GOT IT?

That said, Gentle Reader, if you like to use all capital letters and prefer that your senders use them too because you have limited eyesight, note that you can adjust various settings for your entire computer to help with that. Using all uppercase letters really isn't the best way to improve the readability of something on the screen (not to mention that it isn't the best way to get your point across, especially if your message is something delicate in nature). See the user guide or online help for more information.

# Crab #3: Save the Stationery for Snail Mail

**Note**   For all of you who love to use funky background colors and wild stationery for your personal e-mail, please disregard this crab. This one is for you people at the office. But then again, even if it's personal mail you're sending, read this anyway. Stationery can be...distracting—and that's the nice way of saying it.

I know it's important to you that everyone knows you're creative, arty, and colorful. Your cubicle fairly screams kitsch—how could we not know? But we're at work here, and I don't want to have to hippity-hop through your "bunnies 'n love" stationery just to figure out what your message is. Now, I'm not saying that you shouldn't carefully choose the font, color, and size you want your message to appear in; it's just that a little formatting goes a long way.

I know that Microsoft Office Outlook almost begs you to add color and formatting, and even design your own stationery. (Hey, I've created my own little Crabby Office Lady bullets for mail I send to my coworkers and readers.) But here a few things to consider when deciding on message formatting:

**Color**   Many people have some sort of visual impairment, be it color blindness or the inability to see very well at all. If I were you, I'd stick with plain old black for font color. And if your recipient is using a screen reader (a software program that reads the contents of the screen aloud), colors might just confuse it.

**Fonts**   I like wild and crazy fonts as much as the next gal, but there is a time and a place for them. Creating business cards for my mother's fiber artists business, making art projects with my daughter, and typing up letters to my best friend are all opportunities to get creative with new fonts. Writing e-mail messages at work, however, is not the opportunity to show off your personality (particularly if you're like me, chameleonish and changing every day). We all have a lot to do and a short time to do it in. I just want to be able to read your message and not be distracted by all those funky squiggles, loops, hearts, and dots that your special font employs. So please, stick with one of the usual fonts: Verdana (excellent for on-screen readability), Arial (a little boring but definitely readable), or Courier (again, a bit boring but widely available and easy to read).

**Stationery**    There are a few reasons why I don't like to create or receive e-mail that employs stationery. First, it takes up space, and my e-mail server and I need all the space I can get. Second, some bigger companies might use aggressive e-mail servers that will strip the message to its plain text. (Think of yourself, getting all dressed up for what you thought was a black-tie affair only to find that you were invited to a pool party. Hope you wore clean skivvies!) And last, some of your recipients are receiving mail in plain text, and your stationery will end up looking like gobbledygook anyway.

A final note about stationery and other embellishments: I know that some of you want to spruce up the same-old humdrum formatting that e-mail usually comes in, and so you can. But just use a little discretion, will you? Letterhead is nice, but only if your recipient's mail client is set up to accept images. Many fonts out there are clean, easy to read at various sizes, and won't torture your recipients and burn their corneas. It's your message that's important—remember that. Don't encourage us to kill the messenger.

## Crab #4: The Subject *Re:* Means Nothing to Me

In other words, fill in the Subject line. I get hundreds of e-mail messages each day, and when I get one without anything in the Subject line, I tend to skip over it. If the subject of the message wasn't important enough for the sender to fill in the Subject line, it's not important to me. Begone!

This is a crab near and dear to my heart; I get messages each day from relatives and coworkers who don't take the time to fill in the Subject line. This can be not just annoying but also difficult to deal with when you're trying to organize your e-mail. For example, I like to organize my Inbox by Conversation, and if I've received messages from you as well as other people, messages that didn't have anything in the subject line (just *Re:* over and over again), this makes my organization technique virtually worthless. So, please, think about your recipients and how they might need to refer to your very important message; use the Subject line and make it mean something.

And for you folks whose senders just refuse to use the Subject line, write in something yourself when you reply—something meaningful. If you can't lead a horse to water and make it drink, you can certainly have a snootful yourself and save yourself from dehydration of the Subject line.

## Crab #5: This Is Not a Chain Letter

If I send you a nice note and then get a response from you that, at first glance, appears to have only what I wrote to you at the top of it, I'm going to assume you have nothing to say to me (and sent me an empty e-mail message to tell me as much).

Let's put it this way: when you're replying to an e-mail message and you want to include what the sender wrote, I prefer that you add your comments at the *top* of the mail, not the bottom. I know what I wrote; why would I want to reread it?

That being said, I do see the logic in keeping all the notes and replies in order (my original message on top, followed by your reply, followed by my reply to your reply, and so on). And I know that some of my readers prefer to do it that way, too. Well, it might be like that in the snail mail world, but we're not in Kansas anymore, Toto. Adapt. Your reply on top, please—this isn't a chain letter. (And if it is, don't send it to me. But that's a crab of a different color.)

## Crab #6: Too Many Forwards Is One Step Backward

Speaking of chain letters, if you're like me (and I know you are), you are fed up with receiving the same jokes, Internet rumors, and chain letters promising a free case of champagne, $1,000 from Bill Gates, and miracle cream that erases all your fine lines and bad memories.

Although you can cut some slack for those in your life who have just discovered that Great Oracle of Misinformation we call the Internet, it's just not appropriate, considerate, professional, or even cool to forward these useless things to coworkers. (And by the way: Mikey, the kid from that 1970s-era cereal commercial did not explode after drinking a popular cola laced with fizzy candy. I don't know where he is, but he's probably going through a mid-life crisis right about now.)

Give those people near and dear to you—those who've just discovered the joys of e-mail—a bit of leeway when they start hammering your Inbox with jokes, rumors, and chain letters. Then, when an appropriate amount of time has passed, consider educating them about what constitutes real communication...and what is pure nonsense.

I try to point my friends and family to the various Web sites that are devoted to debunking all the Internet rumors and hoaxes that resurface every few years or so. But we're all human, and we just *want* to believe that we can get something for nothing. We want to trust there is the possibility of free shoes or free beer just by forwarding e-mail messages to 10 of our closest friends or relatives.

But I'm here to let you in on something: it's not true. Think about it, smart friends. How can the champagne company or the restaurant know that you forwarded this e-mail message to exactly nine of your closest e-mail companions? They can't, of course. What can happen, I'm sorry to say, is that when you forward e-mail to a bunch of people, their names and e-mail addresses are visible to anyone, making those addresses very, very, VERY susceptible to the greedy, groping, hungry eyes of spammers. And we all know what spam is, don't we? And we don't want to become (here it comes again) an enabler for a spammer, now do we? Of course we don't. So lay off the forwarded e-mail messages, no matter how exciting, true, or beneficial you might think they are.

## Crab #7: Don't Be a Cyber-Coward

If you have something to say to me that's

- Highly personal
- Scary
- Sad
- Angry
- Tragic
- Vicious
- Shocking
- Any combination of the above

   ...please do it in person. (Actually, I prefer you don't do it at all.) Sentient beings are filled with emotions (and *not* emoticons, those little smiley and frowny faces used to indicate emotion in e-mail). E-mail programs aren't the best conveyors of this.

This is one of the most common ways to abuse e-mail—hiding behind words on a computer screen. While e-mail is one of the best inventions of the 20th century, let me reiterate that it has its bad side. It has become a bit too easy to manically type up a terse response to something someone said that you didn't like, or to pretend to be something you're not (ah, Internet dating).

There is a time and there is a place for e-mail. Firing someone, breaking up with someone, and giving bad news is not when e-mail should take precedence over being a human and doing it in person.

## Crab #8: I Love You but Not Your 500-KB Image File

As I see it, there are three main reasons why you should refrain from sending really large files via e-mail:

**It takes a long time to download a large file.**
> This is particularly true if you are on a dial-up connection. When your recipient is checking e-mail because she's waiting for an important message from the President of the United States (POTUS), it's just plain rude to make her sit there for 10 minutes to download the photo of your dog's birthday party.

**E-mail servers are like studio apartments: there's only so much space to store everything.**
> If your huge file is taking up 3 megabytes (MB) of space on a 4 MB e-mail server, the recipient might ask you to move out, take your stuff, and never come back.

**Sometimes you're at the mercy of the ISP.** Some Internet service providers (ISPs) or
> free e-mail providers limit the size of a single piece of mail coming through their servers. Sometimes this is because of security issues, and sometimes these companies just want to annoy you. Whatever the reason, your recipient might never even know you sent something.

So, please, consider the size of the file you're sending. If it's a large image, make it smaller. If it's a large document, zip it up by using a file compression program. Many image and photo editing software products—even Outlook itself—can help you decide how to resize images for e-mail. Your recipients will thank you, and if they say they want a larger version of your photo or other image, then and only then should you send them that huge file.

## A Smiley Face Emoticon Does Not Disarm a Nasty Comment

If you are saying something unpleasant, adding a little happy face to indicate that you're just kidding just doesn't translate well. Are you indicating that you're being sarcastic? Are you telling me that I should accept your criticism, smile, and move on? Talk to me if the topic is serious, or write *exactly* what you mean. Don't let a combination of keystrokes—colon, dash, right parenthesis—speak for you.

# Crab #9: Plain Text and HTML Are Not Buddies

If someone sends you mail in Plain Text format, you can usually tell because (a) it has no formatting (no bold or italicized words, no lists, no colors or stationery, thank goodness), and (b) the font it appears in is Courier. If you decide to reply to a plain text sender using Hypertext Markup Language (HTML) format with special fonts and formatting, the text that your recipient receives will be almost-indecipherable nonsense that needs a Cold War code breaker to untangle its message. Do your recipients a favor: send your reply in the format the original message came in.

A little bit about the choices you have regarding e-mail message format:

- HTML is the default message format in Outlook. It lets you add formatting for emphasis (not to mention fun—but remember, not *too* much fun) to your message. You can use bold, italics, and hyperlinks. And yes, *most* e-mail programs use HTML as their default format, too. But not all...

Plain Text messages might seem boring to you arty types, but keep in mind that any e-mail program will be able to read your message. (And it's your message that counts...right?)

- Plain Text format is very predictable and, yes, unexciting. However, all e-mail programs understand it. Sure, you can't add color, you can't make anything bold or underlined, and you can't add clickable hyperlinks. But Plain Text has its benefits: it takes the least amount of space on the e-mail server, and anyone can read your message.

- RTF, or Rich Text Format, is the least compatible of these three message formats. One benefit of RTF is that you can show attachments inline—meaning, for example, that a little icon of the Microsoft Office Word document that you're attaching will appear in your message. But honestly, this is useful only if you're sending e-mail to people who are using Outlook with Microsoft Exchange Server. Otherwise, stick to Plain Text or HTML. No one likes gobbledygook.

# Crab #10: Scratch That Itchy Trigger Finger Before Clicking Send

You're impulsive and excitable and everybody knows that (and sometimes loves that) about you. But before sending your clever and scathing message out there to the world (with virtually no chance of retrieving it), remember this: the clicking of the Send button lasts a moment, but its effects can last a lifetime—or at least until you're out on the street, looking for another job.

Now, there is a way to delay that message—kind of like counting to 10 before exploding. (And why am I intimately familiar with this feature? Just guess...) If you want to learn how to delay sending an e-mail message using your particular version of Outlook, refer to the Microsoft Office Online Web site, at office.microsoft.com.

# Manners: Petty Sacrifices

One last thing: I don't want to imply that you can't have fun, be light, or be creative in e-mail. Some of you have gotten to know me since I started writing my Crabby Office Lady column for the Office Online Web site (if you haven't seen it, it's at go.microsoft.com /fwlink/?LinkId=61380) and I'm sure you can imagine that I've had some trouble myself with e-mail etiquette. (No! It's true!) I'm just telling you to think before sending. The job you save may be your own.

## Using the Message Recall Feature

Outlook offers a way to recall the message you so hastily sent...and now want to take back and replace with another. (This feature requires that everyone is on board with Exchange Server.) You can also be notified whether the recall was successful. Exactly how this happens can vary, depending on how your recipient has set up Outlook. But consider this process, which is the most common:

1. Both the original message and the recall message show up in your recipient's Inbox.

2. If the recipient opens the newer message first, he'll be informed that you deleted the original one from his Inbox, and this will pique his interest.

3. If the recipient sees the Subject line of the recalled message (it shouts out "Recalled" right there), chances are, he'll open the original message first to see what was so recallable about it to begin with.

Count to 10 before pushing the Send button. It's your only definitive option for not putting something out there that you didn't really mean to.

Chapter Two

# Demystify Computer Terms and Get On with Your Day

*A man thinks that by mouthing hard words he understands hard things.*

— *Herman Melville*

The lexicon of computing is bloated with terms and phrases that are baffling, if not etymologically strange. And it's come to my attention that some of you (who shall remain nameless, thanks to my own sense of restraint and corporate responsibility) are adrift in this constantly changing world. I believe this isn't your fault, and honestly, sometimes I'm right there with you. I understand that when you're working in a program or trying to get help—using Microsoft Office help, an online support person, or a book—one unknown term or phrase can give you that deer-in-the-headlights sensation, frozen midleap on the highway of knowledge. And then that urge to simply throw up your hands and toss that expensive computer out the window takes precedence over any desire to learn or troubleshoot the issue at hand. Ignorance—when you know you can get out of its tight clutches with the explanation of a single term—is a frustrating state of being. Take a deep breath; I'm here to release you.

# Humans Are Mysterious; Software Terms Needn't Be

Here's how I see it: we human beings may be hard-wired for upright walking, language, and utensil usage, but we still have to learn these skills. And frankly, some of the very smart people who create the software programs that we use every day, or who provide instruction for how to use the software, often forget that they, too, had to learn what those convoluted and complicated terms and acronyms mean. Yes, they had to learn to roll over on their tummies, sit up, and then maybe even crawl before they could start walking and tossing around those terms like so many footballs on a fall afternoon.

At the risk of offending my many coworkers, I need to say right away that some of them—some of *us*—have forgotten who our audience is. It's you, and you just want to be able to do your work—which could mean dealing with e-mail, collaborating with coworkers, calling and attending meetings—and get on with your day. None of us who work in the software industry want to imagine you at your desk, frustrated and angry with the software on which you've spent a good deal of time and money.

To get to the point, I think I know why so many of you have been reticent to jump in and start mail merging and frolicking in the task pane: you have no clue what these things are or how they can give you a better life (or at least free up some of your time).

*Begin the Beguine*, written by Cole Porter, was one of the biggest hits of the Swing Era, particularly for clarinetist Artie Shaw.

So, as the song says, let's "begin the beguine." (What's a *beguine*? Exactly my point: Who knows? Probably very few of you.) There are more terms and acronyms used in the world of computing than you can shake this book at, but I'm going to suss out and demystify some of the more common terms that frighten, irritate, or just plain vex you.

# Ready, Set, Demystify: General Software Terms

Some computer terms and acronyms apply to computers and operating systems in general. It doesn't matter if you're a Microsoft Windows worshipper, an Apple aficionado, or a Linux lover—these are words that you're bound to run across at some point in your computing life:

**Operating system**    The operating system of your computer is the software that makes your computer work. My operating system is Windows; yours might be Windows, Macintosh, or Linux. Software programs—whatever they might be—are designed to work on specific operating systems. For example, Microsoft Office works on both Windows and Macintosh operating systems, but Microsoft Office for Windows and Microsoft Office for Mac are related but completely different products. In other words, you can't buy Office for Windows and expect it to work on your Mac. It's like buying cat booties for a big dog—they won't fit, and therefore won't work, and therefore will embarrass your dog. But you can buy big dog booties (just as you can buy Office for the Macintosh).

**File properties**   The file properties of a document, a presentation, a Web page, or a spreadsheet (or whatever) contain information about that file such as type, size, creation date, and so on. You can usually find this information by clicking Properties on the File menu in a Microsoft Office program. Think of it as a bio and an 8-by-10 headshot for your document.

**BIOS**   Speaking of bios, you may have heard the term *BIOS* being bandied about by a technical support person when your computer stops working (or never worked in the first place). BIOS is an acronym for *basic input/output system*—in simple terms, a set of routines that tests your hardware and gets your operating system going when you start your computer. I think of it as the alarm clock and coffee maker for your computer: when they don't run, you don't run.

**Read-only file**   A read-only file is a document, Web page, spreadsheet, and so on that can only be retrieved (read) and not changed (written). You can tell whether a file is read-only by looking at the file properties (and I *know* you know what that means).

**Macro**   A macro is, in its simplest form, a recording. You perform a series of clicks and actions that make something happen while you're recording them from within a software program. Then you save the recording, to use later. Like a teeny little program unto itself, a macro can save you time by wrapping up a long set of keystrokes, trips to the menu bar, curses, and heavy sighs into a quick key combination or a single click. For example, if you know that you need to enter your name and e-mail address at the bottom of every page in a 32-page document, you can do that by hand once, while you're recording it, and then pop it in on every page using a macro that's started with a single keystroke or two—whatever combination you specify. This is particularly helpful if the note you're adding at the bottom of each page is lengthy.

**Mail merge**   When you do a mail merge, you can put your lists of important things (names, addresses, and so on—some of which might be in a database such as your Microsoft Office Outlook Contacts list) onto letters or envelopes. For this feature, think holiday letters: written, addressed, and sent in one fell swoop. More time for eggnog, I say.

**Dialog box**   A dialog box is a special window displayed by an application and designed to get a response from you. (Hence the word *dialog*.) Usually you have to click, select, or type something in that box to make something show up, change, or go away. (That's right, go away—like Clippy, that misunderstood and often-maligned Microsoft Office Assistant).

**Drag-and-drop**  Drag-and-drop is exactly what it sounds like: picking up something by clicking it with your mouse and then moving it somewhere else by holding down the mouse button and moving the mouse. For example, pick up the icon of that Microsoft Office Word document on your desktop—you know, that fantasy resignation letter to your boss—and drop it in the trash. (Go on—do it now. You'll thank me later.)

**WYSIWYG**  Acronym for *what you see is what you get*. A WYSIWYG program allows you, as the creator of a Web page, for example, to see how the text, images, and links should appear while you're creating the page. Instead of having to know HTML (Hypertext Markup Language, the basic programming language for the Web), you can create Web pages in Microsoft Office FrontPage, a WYSIWYG editor, just as you would write them in a Word document. And it's so fun to say. C'mon, say it with me: WIZZZZZZZZ-eeeeeeee-WIG.

## FrontPage Is Great If You're Not the Technical Type

WYSIWYG, a way to create Web pages by seeing exactly how your text, images, and links will appear, is a great method for those who can't take the time to learn HTML, the language of the Internet. You just design your pages to your heart's content, and FrontPage will take care of the rest. Think of it as your own personal translator.

**Plug-and-play**  Ah...my favorite kind of hardware. You just plug it into your computer and you're good to go. Technically, plug-and-play is a set of specifications that allows your computer to set itself up automatically to work with hardware such as monitors, modems, and printers. It's just as it sounds: plug it in and go...usually without having to turn your computer on and off. (Who needs that aggravation and waste of time? Don't you wish more things in your life—your spouse, your child, your DVD player—were plug-and-play? Or at least plug-yourself-in-and-let-me-be?)

**Mouse pointer**   The mouse pointer is that thing with which you point. No, not your finger. You know—the pointy cursor thing you move around on your screen with the mouse.

**Bug**   A bug is a flaw in a program or system. While the folks at Microsoft surely strive to send out bug-free products, they are, after all, humans, and some things get past the error checkers. There are people like you to let them know about bugs so that they can fix the bug either next time around (in the next version) or through an update. I think of a bug as a hole or tear in your jeans—you don't need a new pair; you just need a little piece of fabric and a needle and thread. (Or, in my case, a press-on patch and an iron. I'm not much of a needle-and-thread gal.)

# Ready, Set, Demystify: Working-in-the-Office Program Terms

You're furiously working in an Office program that's acting as your partner for a particular project. If you don't understand how to use the features built in to make you more efficient, you'll end up spending more time researching the basics than working on what really counts: your document.

**Shortcut menu**   When you right-click anywhere, a little menu called the shortcut menu pops up. It has a list of actions to choose from, and it's usually short. (Good name for it, eh?) Some of the options on a shortcut menu are Cut, Copy, Paste, Forward, Delete, and so on. It really just depends on what you're right-clicking.

**Keyboard shortcut**   Also referred to as the *shortcut key*, a keyboard shortcut is a special combination of key presses (using the keyboard) that causes something to happen. For example, if you hold down the CTRL key and then press the A key, everything in your document, Web page, spreadsheet, or whatever will be selected.

To find a list of all keyboard shortcuts in a program, press F1 to open Help, and then search for **keyboard shortcuts**. Crazy, easy as pie,...but true. Keyboard shortcuts are not just for fun; they are also a big part of what makes a program accessible. For more information, see Chapter 9, "Ergonomics and Accessibility: Making It Easier on Yourself (and Others)."

If you prefer to use your keyboard instead of your mouse, keyboard shortcuts are your best friends. And you can even customize them to suit your needs. (See Chapter 3, "Go Ahead and Nest: Customizing Office.")

**ScreenTip**   You know that little yellow box that pops up when you hold the mouse pointer over a toolbar button or a hyperlink? The little message that pops up tells you about that item. That little message is a ScreenTip.

**Task pane**   Located on the right side of an application window and present when you first start a Microsoft Office program or click Task Pane on the View menu, the task pane frees you from those repeated trips to the menu bar and from having to scroll through lists of actions (that is just *so* last century). Different programs offer different types of task panes (such as the Insert Clip Art, Styles And Formatting, and Clipboard task panes). You can switch from one to the other by clicking the drop-down arrow at the top of the task pane.

Yes, you can turn off the task pane so that it doesn't appear every time you open a Microsoft Office program. On the Tools menu, click Options, and then click the View tab. Clear the Startup Task Pane check box. If you want to reopen the task pane (and you *will* want to), press CTRL+F1, and the same task pane you used most recently will appear.

**Menu bar**   The menu bar is the rectangular bar displayed in a program's window, usually at the top, from which you can select menus. It's a bit like that box of to-go menus at a restaurant that you browse through while you're waiting to be seated.

**Menu**    A menu is a list of options on the menu bar from which you can choose an action to perform. (The action—cut, paste, format, check spelling—is called a *menu command.*) Think of menus at a restaurant: the lunch menu lets you choose from those things having to do with lunch, the kiddie menu is for the kids (and the cheapskates), and the wine menu is for those of you ready to step outside the box. (The wine box, that is—are you paying attention?)

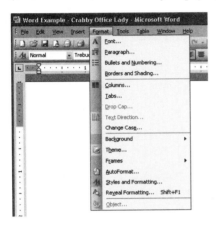

**Toolbar**    A toolbar (and there are many different types) is a bar with buttons and options that you can use to carry out the job at hand. You'll find a list of toolbars available to you on the View menu. Some examples are the Formatting toolbar, the Drawing toolbar, and the Mail Merge toolbar. You can also create your own toolbar, one that really carries out your deepest computing wishes. To do this, on the View menu, point to Toolbars, and then click Customize. Then go wild, go crazy, make it your own.

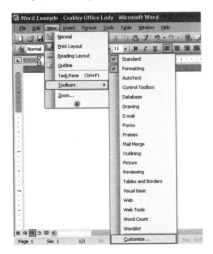

# Ready, Set, Demystify: E-Mail Terms

As you know (especially after reading Chapter 1), everybody is using e-mail these days. And sure, it's pretty easy to set up an account and start sending and receiving messages. But there are some technical terms that could make your time spent with e-mail more efficient, if you understood them. I'm here for you.

**E-mail client**   An e-mail client is the software program on your computer that enables you to send, receive, and work with e-mail. Examples of e-mail clients are Microsoft Office Outlook, Outlook Express, and Entourage. Which e-mail client you use has nothing to do with your e-mail. If you change clients, you're not changing e-mail addresses. (Dad? Are you reading this?) This is, for some reason, a very hard concept to make clear. An e-mail client (or program) is just the little gremlin inside your computer that brings you your incoming e-mail messages and sends your outgoing messages to your intended recipients. And you, being the computer owner, get to choose which gremlin that is.

**Domain name**   In e-mail, a domain name is the part of an e-mail address that comes after the @ sign. My e-mail address is crabby@microsoft.com, so my domain name is microsoft.com. Yours might be hotmail.com, msn.com, or *(your own obscure name)*.com. Your domain name identifies one or more Internet Protocol (IP) addresses (assigned numbers that identify computers on the network). Each domain name has a top-level domain it belongs to, such as .com (commercial), .edu (education), .gov (government), .org (usually a nonprofit organization, but not always), .mil (the military), and some newer ones such as .biz., .tv, .name, and .pro.

**Protocol**   Usually, when I hear the word *protocol*, what comes to my mind are mustachioed men and smartly dressed women speaking tactfully in multiple languages at a head-of-state dinner party. Typically, the word means "rules or conventions of correct behavior on official or ceremonial occasions." (Thanks, MSN Encarta.)

While we're not talking about diplomacy (not really my specialty, as you may have guessed), there *is* a connection between the ceremony and etiquette that diplomats specialize in and the way e-mail works. In fact, when we talk about an e-mail protocol, we're talking about an agreed-upon format for sending and receiving e-mail messages. And when you think about it, dealing with e-mail can be likened to establishing relations between world leaders: protocol and etiquette are of the utmost importance.

Now that that's as clear as mud, why should you care? You should care because unless you know what protocol your e-mail provider supports, you won't be sure about how to set up Outlook, Outlook Express, or any other e-mail program. And then you won't be able to get your mail, and then where will you be?

Therefore, to send e-mail to and from different kinds of e-mail servers, we need an agreed-upon format for sending and receiving the data. This format is called the protocol, and there are a few types—POP3, IMAP, HTTP mail, and MAPI are the most common.

**POP3**   When you use the very common Post Office Protocol 3 (POP3), your e-mail is stored on your e-mail provider's server initially. But once you retrieve your e-mail with Outlook, Outlook Express, or whatever e-mail program you use, it's downloaded—or moved—to your computer and is no longer stored on the server. If you want to keep an e-mail message, you can either never delete it from your e-mail program or create a copy of it and keep it somewhere on your computer (and hopefully you're better at remembering where you put it than I am).

Most Internet service providers (ISPs) deliver mail to you using the POP3 protocol for a few reasons. POP3 provides security since your messages are not stored on the ISP's server (unlike IMAP and HTTP mail, which we'll be getting to in a minute). When you sign up for an account with an ISP, the ISP gives you an allotment of server space to store your messages. If all of your messages are kept on the server, it's possible that the one critical message that you need to get is bounced back to the sender because you've run out of server space. What's more, you don't have to be connected to the Internet to be able to read your e-mail. POP3 is also the best protocol when you have one computer and you want to store all your mail on that computer.

**IMAP**   Internet Message Access Protocol (IMAP) is a way to access your e-mail on a server. E-mail messages are stored on the network instead of on your local computer.

IMAP is a useful type of protocol to use when you have multiple computers and you want to be able to access your e-mail from any one of them And it's also useful if you want to view just the headers of your messages and then decide whether you want to download them. (There's no need to download an entire spam message when the header is shocking enough.) Also, if you're the superorganized type and you like to create and move folders or entire mailboxes and even search for certain parts of a message, IMAP is the protocol for you.

While this is all well and good, not all e-mail providers support IMAP. So before you get all excited, I'd check with them.

Figure out which protocol works best for your e-mailing situation before deciding on the provider you want to go with. Having choices is always a good thing.

**HTTP mail**   Hypertext Transfer Protocol (HTTP) is used to display Web pages, but it can also be used to send and receive e-mail.

You'll be using HTTP mail when you have an account with MSN, Hotmail, Yahoo!, or any other Web-based e-mail service. The benefit of this type of protocol is that you can read and receive e-mail messages from any computer in the world with an Internet connection and a Web browser that supports graphics. When you're using Microsoft Exchange Server and Microsoft Office Outlook Web Access (OWA), you'll also be using HTTP mail. With OWA, you can get all your mail, contacts, and calendar information on the server by using an Internet browser from a computer running UNIX, Macintosh, or Microsoft Windows. For remote connections, you can also use HTTP to connect from Outlook to a computer running Microsoft Exchange Server using a feature called *Remote Procedure Call (RPC) over HTTP*. (Sexy name, isn't it?) This is an alternative to the standard virtual private network (VPN) connection

HTTP accounts are not as private as POP3 accounts because your messages are stored on an external server. Also, the amount of space you get to store messages is limited; if you go over that set amount, you won't be able to get or send more messages until you clean out your closet (thereby making room for more new clothes).

**MAPI**   Messaging Application Programming Interface (MAPI) is used with Outlook in conjunction with a mail server running Microsoft Exchange Server. MAPI is a lot like IMAP (it's not just an anagram of it), but it provides a wider array of features when you use it from within Outlook. In fact, MAPI makes it possible for other Microsoft Office programs (such as Word and Excel) to work with your e-mail program.

Use MAPI when you want to develop new types of custom forms or you need your e-mail program (such as Outlook) to work with another program (such as Word)—for example, if you want to access your Outlook Contacts folder for a mail merge you're setting up in Word. MAPI is also a useful protocol when you want to use profiles to configure how an e-mail message is transmitted and where it is stored. Another, and possibly the biggest reason, to use MAPI: your organization uses Outlook with Exchange Server and you have no choice in the matter.

**Incoming mail server**   When you're setting up an e-mail account in Outlook (or in any e-mail program), you'll need to specify the incoming mail server. This server is where your incoming mail is stored before you go and get it. You'll need to contact your e-mail provider to find out what your incoming mail server is, because you'll be asked for that information when you're setting up your account the first time.

**Outgoing mail server**   Your outgoing mail server is used to send e-mail messages only—not to receive them. Most outgoing mail servers use Simple Mail Transfer Protocol (SMTP) for sending e-mail messages. When you set up your e-mail client with your e-mail information, your outgoing mail server might (but not always) start with smtp.*your mail server*.com.

**SMTP**   While most (but not all) e-mail systems use POP3 to transfer incoming messages to you, most (but not all) e-mail systems use SMTP to send e-mail messages across the Internet, from your e-mail client to someone else's e-mail server. That's why you need to specify both the incoming server (POP3, IMAP, and so on) and the outgoing server (the SMTP server) when you set up your e-mail accounts.

**Exchange Server**   Exchange Server is an e-mail-based collaborative communications server for business. Got that? In plain terms, it's a messaging system—one that allows you to send and receive mail, keep your messages on the server, keep your contacts on the server, and see your calendar and your coworkers' calendars so that you can see when they're free for the long meeting you plan on calling to fill their afternoon. Exchange is mostly used for large organizations. Your e-mail client—Outlook on your workstation, or your Pocket PC, or your mobile phone—connects to a network of computer systems where your e-mail is stored. This allows everyone to collaborate—Exchange is all about collaboration. Chances are, if you're a home user, you don't use (or need) Exchange Server. Again, it's mostly used by businesses that need those heavy-duty collaboration features.

**Above the fold**   Refers to the portion of an e-mail message (or Web page, or newspaper, or any written or typed content, actually) that is visible without scrolling down the page or screen. In newspapers, the most important content is above the fold so that readers can see it right away without having to unfold the paper. It's kind of tricky to predict where the fold is in e-mail messages because there are so many variables that you can't control, such as your recipients' screen resolution and font size.

**Attachment**   An image, a video or audio file, or any other sort of data file that is sent along with (or attached to) an e-mail message.

**Bounces**   Bounces are messages that can't reach their destination and are returned to you, the sender. There are *hard bounces* (due to invalid e-mail addresses) and *soft bounces* (due to temporary conditions, such as full Inboxes.) In either case, your message didn't reach its recipients.

**Message header**   Message headers provide a list of technical details, such as whom the message came from, the software used to compose it, and the e-mail servers it passed through on the way to you, the recipient. These details can be useful for identifying problems with e-mail or identifying sources of spam.

**Subject line**   The use (or non-use) of the Subject line is Crabby's second biggest e-mail pet peeve (the first being the Bcc line—see below). The Subject line is where you put the, um, subject of your e-mail message. Sending messages without anything in the Subject line is like writing a book without a title: just don't do it.

**Cc**   The Cc line is directly below the To line in an e-mail message. *Cc* stands for *carbon copy*, and everyone on that list will get an exact copy of the e-mail message that you or anyone else sends. Use the Cc line when you want to send the message to people who aren't the biggest stakeholders in the conversation that might ensue. If the recipient clicks Reply, his or her message will be sent only to you, the sender. If the recipient clicks Reply All, everyone in the To and Cc lines will receive a copy of the message.

---

**Note**   If you've read Chapter 1, which covers e-mail etiquette, you know that the clicking of Reply All is one of my biggest e-mail crabs.

---

**Bcc**   If you're already familiar with the Crabby Office Lady, you know that the Bcc line is near and dear to my crabby heart. In case you're still in the dark about what *Bcc* stands for, it's *blind carbon copy*. When you add someone's e-mail address to the Bcc line, a copy of your message is sent to that person but the address will not be visible to anyone else receiving the message (hence the "blind" part of it).

Using the Bcc line to prevent the spread of e-mail addresses over all digital kingdom come is all well and good, but it's up to the sender to instigate it. (And perhaps, even to educate the people to whom you're Bcc-ing. A little exemplary behavior can go a long way.) See, when you're sending out a mass mailing (a joke, a rumor, and other types of mails I've already told you to try and avoid) and you want to protect the e-mail addresses and identities of everyone on that mailing, use the Bcc line. Think of it this way (and I'll try and keep this is as G-rated as I can): when A kisses B and then B kisses C, it's just as if C kissed A (creating a real rift between B and C, but that's a different sort of advice for a different sort of book).

In case you've forgotten the correct usage of the Bcc line, let's just have a little reminder session about when it's appropriate to use Bcc—and when it's not:

- When you don't want someone on the To or Cc line to know that you are including another person in that message, put that other person's address in the Bcc box. Yes, this is sneaky, but it's useful in certain circumstances.

- Let's say you begin to see an e-mail conversation, which includes many people, starting to get really heated and long. If you understand that some of the recipients simply don't need to be in on the conversation any longer, when it's your turn to reply, put these people's address in the Bcc box and then put a little message at the top of your reply indicating that you're doing so. These people will heave a huge sigh of relief and thank you later.

**MIME and S/MIME**   Multipurpose Internet Mime Extensions (MIME) extends the basic, text-oriented Internet mail system. It provides a way to format a message so that you can include non-alphanumeric characters and nontext content such as a picture file. The message can then be sent over the Internet to people using all kinds of e-mail clients, protocols, and text editors. Secure/MIME (S/MIME) supports encrypted (secret-coded) messages—that's what Outlook uses when it's used in conjunction with Microsoft Exchange Server.

# Ready, Set, Demystify: Getting Online

You're finally joining the digital age: you're getting online. The barrage of choices you need to make and how you make them can put a real damper on your enthusiasm in your endeavor. What hardware and software will you need? Which companies offer which services? Do your neighborhood cable and phone lines support your method of choice? Knowing what your options are and what they mean can make the process go a lot more smoothly.

**Bandwidth**   Refers to how quickly information travels to and from your computer. It's usually expressed in bits per second (bps), kilobits per second (Kbps), or megabits per second (Mbps).

**DSL**   Stands for *Digital Subscriber Line*. DSL is a technology that brings high-speed (or high-bandwidth) transfer of information over ordinary copper telephone lines. A DSL line can carry both

## Finding the Right ISP for You

When you're researching Internet service providers (ISPs), be sure to ask the company whether it provides spam filters and virus protection. If you're paying good money for e-mail and Internet access, these options should be available to you.

data and voice signals (and the data part of the line is continuously connected) so you can use your computer and your phone at the same time.

**Dial-up**  Describes when a modem is used to connect to the Internet via a network. When you have a dial-up connection, you're using your telephone—a device meant to carry voice messages. It's the slowest—and cheapest—way to connect to the Internet.

**Broadband**  A term that refers to high-speed, high-capacity Internet and data connections—connections that are always on. Broadband uses wide-bandwidth channels for sending and receiving large amounts of information. Broadband is generally taken to mean bandwidth higher than 2 Mbps. Cable, satellite, and DSL connections use broadband.

# Ready, Set, Demystify: Nasty Things in E-Mail

Okay. You're online, you're connected, you've set up your e-mail account, and you've sent out your new e-mail address to everyone you know. Congratulations! Now the real fun begins. You *must* learn what scary things are lurking out there, just waiting to get you, and possibly hose your brand-new system and use your e-mail address to send out pornographic messages and spam to entrap your friends and family into...heaven knows what.

But never fear—if you're aware of the dangers, you'll be prepared to fight back...with knowledge.

**Spam**  Spam is unsolicited e-mail, commercial or otherwise. No one is completely safe from spam, but it sure is a hotbed of conversation. Some anti-spam legislation has recently passed, but it's ridiculously hard to enforce it.

**Virus**  A virus is a software program whose sole purpose is to cause problems for your computer. A computer virus behaves similarly to a human virus: it causes mischief by inserting itself into an existing living organism (in this case, your computer). It's usually disguised as something else, and it's often transmitted as an e-mail attachment or a download.

**Worm**  A worm is a self-replicating computer program, similar to a computer virus. The difference is that a virus attaches itself and becomes a part of another program, but a computer worm, just like the soft-bodied invertebrate animal, is self-replicating. It propagates through the Internet and through e-mail and can be very destructive to the computers that are infected, by altering, installing, or destroying files and programs. A worm likes to make itself at home in your computer's memory. (I guess it's wet and slimy there.)

**Flame mail**  A *flame* is an intentionally crude, rude, or offensive e-mail message, newsgroup post, or mailing list message. *Flame wars* occur when a series of flames are sent back and forth between two or more people. In my opinion, we have enough wars going without creating some online.

**Spoofing**   When you are spoofing (and I know you wouldn't dare), you're attempting to gain access to a Web site or an e-mail account by posing as an authorized user. Shame on you!

**Phishing**   Phishing scams try to get personal information from you for identity theft. Any e-mail you get about foreign lotteries, about PayPal trying to get you to update your personal information, or about money in Nigeria that someone needs help getting out of the country is a phishing scam. Don't bite the phishing line; you may end up with a painful hook in your mouth that may take years to heal. Phishing is a form of Internet fraud that aims to steal valuable information such as credit card numbers, social security numbers, user IDs, and passwords. For example, you could get an e-mail message you assume to be from your bank, asking you to log on to their Web site and verify your account name, password, bank account number, and so on. But the Web site, which looks completely legitimate, is a fake. It's a "spoofed" site. (I read that phishing is spelled the way it is because hackers have a tendency to replace *f* with *ph*. Phancy that!)

**Harvesting**   Harvesting (and I don't know about you, but this term gives me visions of sci-fi alien movies) is an illegal practice of using an automated program to scan Web pages and collect e-mail addresses for use by spammers and phishers.

# Ready, Set, Demystify: The Difference Between...

Sometimes it's hard to distinguish between certain terms or phrases when it comes to computerese. But if you don't understand the distinctions between these terms, you may one day find yourself either buying a computer system that isn't right for you or (heaven forbid) talking to a customer support person or client who doesn't understand the issue.

**Server and client**   A server is a computer or program that responds to commands from the client. The server is like the generous-but-judicious big-ole granddaddy of the computer family. All wisdom flows from him to various children, grandchildren, and bocce ball buddies. An example of an e-mail server is Exchange Server.

The client is the grandchild of the granddaddy server: it's a computer that accesses files, software downloads, dusty old records, birthday checks, and other shared items provided by another computer (the server). An example of an e-mail client is Outlook.

**Themes, style sheets, and cascading style sheets**  A *theme* is a set of design elements and color schemes that you can apply to your Web pages, documents, publications, spreadsheets, and databases to give them a professional, playful, or personal look. FrontPage, for example, comes with several preinstalled themes, and you can download more as well. You can change parts of existing themes to create a new theme (such as deciding you want links to be green instead of red). And as we've all witnessed, good taste is not a requirement for applying themes to Web pages. (Of course, themes can be applied to Word documents, PowerPoint presentations, Publisher brochures, and so on.)

A *style sheet* is a file that's associated with and defines the layout of a document or Web page. To create a style sheet, you specify such things as fonts, page numbering, margins, and so on. Then you apply the style sheet—or link it —to your Web page. A style sheet is similar to a theme; it's really a set of rules that follows the page around—the fashion police of the Web page world. A style sheet is also a template.

A cascading style sheet gives you more control over how the Web pages you create are displayed in the various viewers' browsers. You create style sheets that define how different elements—such as the various types of text, headers, hyperlinks, and background colors—appear in your Web pages. The term *cascading* is used because you can apply more than one style sheet to a page. Cascading also sounds better than dripping, spilling, or falling over.

**RAM and ROM**  The physical memory of a computer, the amount of information it can hold and process at one time, is either read-only memory (ROM) or random access memory (RAM):

**ROM**  Just like its name intimates, you can't change any information that is stored in ROM—it's predefined and preset when you buy a computer. You need ROM—it keeps the essential information about operating your computer. In fact, the BIOS is usually stored in ROM (and I *know* you know what the BIOS is.)

**RAM**  When you talk about upgrading the memory of your computer, you're talking about the RAM memory. RAM memory holds data and programs for immediate use so that the more RAM you have, the quicker you'll be able to access these programs, and the more programs you'll be able to have open at one time.

**Rumba and beguine**  A *rumba* is a ballroom dance in 4/4 time. Its origins are Cuban. A *beguine* is a ballroom dance similar to the rumba, but the accent is on the second eighth note. Make sure you can count before attempting it.

# Yes, the Terms Are Never-Ending

There are just way too many terms, acronyms, and phrases that you really should know—that I'm really desperate for you to know—because if you want to move forward with this whole computer, Internet, and e-mail thing, we have to all be on the same page. So promise that if you come across a term that leaves you dumbstruck, you'll look it up. There are a thousand Web sites devoted to describing what all these things mean (Encarta being just one), and it's easy enough to find them.

But now you know a bit more than you did when you fell headlong into this chapter. So stop giving me that blank Botox stare and get on with your life, and for heaven's sake, get outside and get some sun, will you?

Chapter Three

# Go Ahead and Nest: Customizing Office

*Style is the mind skating circles around itself while it moves forward.*

— *Robert Frost*

Whether you're conventional or conceptual, strait-laced or silly, you can make Microsoft Office look and work the way you want it to. Let's customize your Office programs to suit your way of working and your delicate sensibilities.

# What Does *Default* Mean?

When you first install Office (or if it came preinstalled on that brand-spankin'-new computer you bought), its settings—toolbars, buttons, your working folder, the template that opens when you create a new document, spreadsheet, or whatever—are installed and set up in one specific way, known as the *default* settings. For example, some toolbars are already showing and some aren't; font sizes, font styles, and colors are also already picked for you; and the Normal template, the one that the designers assume you want to use (ohhhhh....never assume) is also already set up. These default settings are the ones that will remain as they are...unless *you* change them.

And that's my point: you can change them. And frankly, you *should* change them. I mean, why not? We all have our own personal sense of style (whether or not we admit to it), and these styles—these choices—should not be left by the wayside when it comes to working in Office. Because if you (like me) spend a good portion of your workday toiling away in Microsoft Office Word, Excel, PowerPoint, Outlook, or any other Office program (or any program, for that matter), it's a good idea to feel at home, to feel like you're working in an atmosphere that you're comfortable in, don't ya think? Now, you might want to keep some of the default settings, and that's okay, too. It doesn't mean that you're uncreative; it just means that you like what was given to you, and why fix what ain't broke, right? Right. Sometimes simplicity is the path of least resistance. But sometimes it isn't...

Let me put this into a familiar scenario. Take a little quiz with me, won't you?

When you go on a trip and you arrive at your hotel, which of the following scenarios best describes what you do?

A. Throw your suitcase on the bed, splash some water on your face, and head out the door to explore the area.

B. Throw your suitcase on the bed, change your clothes, check out the minibar, splash some water on your face, and head out the door to explore the area.

C. Throw your suitcase on the bed, open the drapes, and then unpack, unfold, and put away every item. Prop up some framed photos, see what's in the minibar, check out the cable guide, review the fire evacuation plan, pocket all the free lotion and shampoo bottles right away, and note the checkout time in your Pocket PC. Take a long hot bath, have a dreamless snooze, brush, floss, splash cold water on your face, and head out the door to explore the area.

D. Forget the hotel—you're happy in a yurt!

Don't be afraid to change the options that came pre-loaded with your Office programs. This is not a one-size-fits-all world we live in (digital or otherwise).

If you said A, settle down, cha-cha—the world can wait. The hotel room is part of the trip. If you said B, you're on the right track—you know how to stop and smell the roses. But you're still just accepting what's already been prepared for you. If you chose C, you're experiencing nesting overload, but that doesn't mean you're overly controlling. (Stick with me—I can help.)

And D? I'd like to see you and C on a honeymoon together. What a great tale to tell your kids (if you make it that far).

So what does this scenario have to do with customizing your Office products? Simple: it shows how comfortable you like to get with your surroundings. Are you happy with the standard toolbar, the buttons all lined up like little soldiers, just taking things as they come? Or are you more inclined to add personal touches and make the place feel like home immediately?

So, what I'm saying here is that it's okay to be needy; it's just fine if you don't like what was handed to you at the installation point—the default settings. I like a bit of creativity, a little bit of refashioning, and I want you to be comfortable working in the Office programs. Why shouldn't you be? Comfy people are happy, productive people. (At least, that's what they tell us, and so far, it's worked pretty well.)

> Meet my parents, D and C. After more than 40 years, they've worked it out and are still happy as clams together. (And no, I didn't grow up in a yurt.)

# Go Ahead: Be Needy

So...what do you need? Maybe you want really large, really wide drop-down lists that take up half your screen. Or maybe you just don't feel fulfilled until every single toolbar and toolbar button available to modern humanity is up there, standing tall, and available to you at all times.

Whatever your needs, Office is ready for you to settle in. And the easiest way for us to get started is for me to pick up your bags, take you up the elevator, hold my hand out for a tip, and open the blinds for you so that you can see the view. Ready? Let's check in and see what this software suite offers in the way of amenities.

There are lots of little things you can do to make your Office window friendlier and easier to use. I mean, some of you spend an awful lot of time fiddling with menus, buttons, and toolbars. If I know my readers, I've lost you already on the difference between menu, button, and toolbar. Let me see if I can remedy that quickly.

# Menus, Buttons, and Toolbars (Oh My!)

I'm going to cut to the chase right away and define what these things are. Ready? Open up Word, Excel, Outlook, PowerPoint, or whatever Office program you're most comfortable in and follow along.

**Title bar**   The title bar, across the top of the window, is what displays the name of your document or the program you're working in. When I open a new Word document, the title bar reads *Doc1 – Microsoft Word*.

**Menu bar**   The menu bar is below the title bar and contains the names of menus, such as File, Edit, View, and Insert. (Different programs have different menus, but the preceding ones are standard.)

**Menu command**   A menu command is an instruction that you want to give your Office program (such as Save, Print, and Open). A menu command is located on a menu. (Seems straightforward enough, no?)

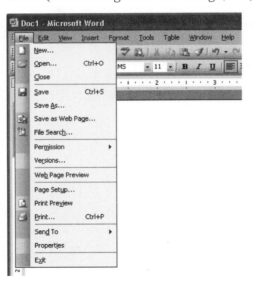

**Toolbar**  A toolbar is a bar (usually below the menu bar) with buttons and options that you use to carry out commands. You can use the View menu to specify which toolbars you want to show—for example, the Drawing toolbar, Formatting toolbar, Forms toolbar, and so on.

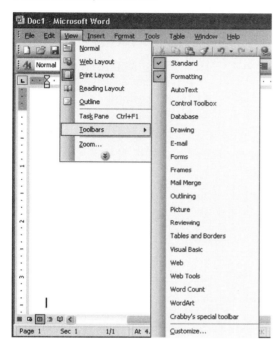

**Button**  A button is a graphical element that performs a specific function. It's similar to a menu command, but it's in graphical format. There are buttons for just about anything—Save, Spelling And Grammar, and Format Painter are just a few. A set of buttons make up a toolbar.

Now that you know what some of these things mean, let me tell you how you can pick and choose which toolbars, buttons, and menus you really need to use on a regular basis. You can set up your window so that they are right there, at your fingertips.

## A Little Bit About Menus

When you first install an Office program and you click a menu (remember, such as File, Edit, or View), only the basic menu commands appear—things like Save (on the File menu), Copy (on the Edit menu), or Print Layout (on the View menu). The rest of the available commands are hidden behind the double down arrow; you have to click that arrow to make the rest of the commands appear.

## Pick a Toolbar...Any Toolbar

Different Office programs offer different toolbars. For example, Excel offers the External Data and Formula Auditing toolbars, while FrontPage wouldn't know what to do with such things. FrontPage has the DHTML Effects and the Navigation toolbars, while Visio would scratch its head and wonder, for all eternity, what *DHTML* means (as, maybe, you would).

You probably don't want to see all of the available toolbars all the time. Sometimes you'll want only the Formatting toolbar up there, and at other times, you'll be interested in just the Formula or Drawing toolbar. Guess what? You can pick the toolbars you want to view.

To choose the toolbars you want to show:

- On the **View** menu, point to **Toolbars**, and then click the toolbar you want.

Seems simple, doesn't it? Well, it is. You just need to take the time to do it. Same goes for the other ways you can customize how your window is set up.

Maybe, for the most part, you like the Formatting toolbar but don't really need the Font Color or even the Highlight button hogging space. Or maybe you want just one button—say, the Check Box button on the Forms toolbar—there at your disposal. You can even create a customized toolbar, one that has only the buttons you use on a regular basis. To make these changes, follow these steps:

1. On the **Tools** menu, click **Customize**.
2. In the Customize dialog box, click the **Toolbars** tab.
3. Click **New**.
4. In the **Toolbar name** box, type the name you want, and then click **OK**. The new toolbar might be *docked*, meaning that it's already sitting with the other toolbars; more likely, it's a small box *floating* somewhere on the screen. If you want it to be docked, nice and pretty, with the other toolbars, drag its title bar or handle to where you want it—the toolbar will snap into place.

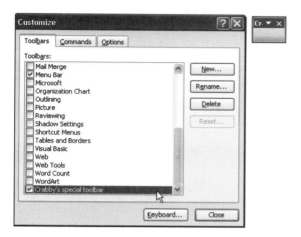

5. In the Customize dialog box, click the **Commands** tab.

6. Click a category in the **Categories** list.

7. Drag the command you want from the **Commands** list to the toolbar you just created. Or drag the button you don't want off the toolbar.

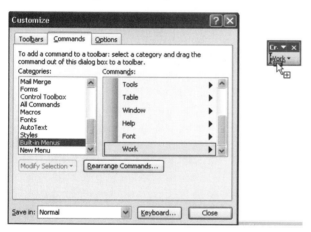

8. When you have added or removed all the buttons and menus you want, click **Close**.

And there you have it: your very own toolbar, customized to suit your needs.

## Button, Button, Who Has the Button?

The Microsoft Office program designers have chosen button icons that make sense. For example, the Save button looks like a little disk. The Open button looks like a little folder that's opening. Seems simple enough. But if you want to get creative and assign different pictures to buttons—even if just for the pure fun of it—you can.

1. On the **Tools** menu, click **Customize**.

2. In the **Customize** dialog box, click the **Commands** tab, and then click the button on the toolbar that you want to modify.

3. Click **Modify Selection**, point to **Change Button Image**, and then click an image. Or make another choice, such as **Text only** or **Image and text**.

Now that you've made the toolbars and their button images look the way you want, it's on to bigger things: working with the Normal template and using the AutoCorrect tools so that you save time and energy.

## Why Be Normal?

When you open a new Word document, Excel spreadsheet, or PowerPoint presentation, it's the Normal template that opens. You might not see anything on that blank page, but there is a lot going on there. The margins are set; font styles, sizes, and colors are there; and things such as toolbars, AutoText, and other customizations are there, too—things that determine the look of your document even before you type a single letter. The software designers created this "normal" template so that you wouldn't have to make a lot of choices right off the bat. A blank page is one thing, and as a writer, I know the dread, the fear, and the whiteness of a blank page. But when you open an Office document, these little choices that have already been made let you get started on whatever it is you're doing (or spending hours and hours contemplating doing).

### *Normal* Means Different Things to Different People

Making your Normal template feel *normal* for you is easy, painless, and ultimately useful. And while it isn't permanent (things rarely are), you will have to go through the steps all over again if you want to return to the default Normal template or if you decide that what was *normal* yesterday isn't *normal* today.

However, maybe the choices of margins, fonts, or whatever just don't agree with you. Maybe they give you indigestion; maybe they spiral you toward a psychotic episode. (In this last case, perhaps you're taking this all a little too seriously. Close your laptop and go do some yoga, read a book, or play with your kids. This isn't life or death—or at least it shouldn't be.)

If you want to change the Normal template—if your sense of normal isn't what this template is providing you—you can change it (and by now, you should know that). It's not a particularly long procedure to change the Normal template, but it doesn't make for exciting reading, so I'm going to direct you to the Office Online Web site (office.microsoft.com). Type **Change Normal template** in the Search box, and you'll see an article that will guide you through the process. Note that this isn't about using a template one time or even a few times; this procedure will change, for good, the main template that opens each time you create a new document, spreadsheet, presentation, or whatever. So make your choices wisely. Sometimes the gifts we've been given should not be disregarded. (I just made that up.)

## AutoCorrect Is My Autopilot

And now on to one of my all-time favorite features in any program: AutoCorrect. First I'll explain what it is, and then I'll tell you how you can make your own AutoCorrect entries that, if you work mainly in Word, for example, will work in any other Office program. In other words, define an AutoCorrect option one time in one program, and you won't have to do it again.

But I'm getting ahead of myself. I promised you an explanation, and here it is: "To automatically detect and correct typos, misspelled words, and incorrect capitalization, you can use AutoCorrect." (This is directly from the help topic titled "About automatic corrections," written by one of my coworkers.) But that isn't the whole story. Oh, no—if it were, I wouldn't be so excited about it (and I'm not the excitable type, I can tell you that).

### AutoCorrect Is Your Ticket to Fast Typing

You can use the AutoCorrect feature to automatically correct your bad spelling and mistyping, thereby saving you time and embarrassment. But you can also train AutoCorrect to type long phrases, acronyms, and symbols that you have neither the time nor inclination to type yourself. This doesn't constitute sloth—go ahead and count it as efficiency doing its work.

First do me a favor: Open Word (any document or none at all). On the Tools menu (which I hope you still have up there; it really is quite useful), click AutoCorrect Options. Now, about in the middle of that window, look where it says Replace and then next to that, With. Below that is a list of a bunch of AutoCorrect options. For example, (c) is replaced with ©. That means that whenever you type **(c)**, Word will replace it with the copyright symbol. Cool, eh?

Maybe not. Maybe you don't want Office to replace what you type. In that case, click that entry, and then click Delete. If you have a list of things that you know you want to replace with something else, now's the time to do it.

Now for the fun part. Let's say that you have a phrase that you have to type repeatedly. For example, today I had to keep typing **Small Business Accounting** all day long (long story—don't ask). I decided, after the fifth or sixth time (I can be a little hard-headed, even for a lousy typist), to create my own AutoCorrect entry. And here's how:

1. On the **Tools** menu, I clicked **AutoCorrect Options**.

2. In the **Replace** box, I typed **SBA**. In the **With** box, I typed **Small Business Accounting**.

3. Then I gleefully clicked **Add**.

Now, whenever I type **SBA**, Word magically turns it into *Small Business Accounting*.

But that's not all—no, that's not all. Suppose you're constantly misspelling a word, and frankly, you're sick of making the same error. You can *train* your Office program to correct that misspelling (and you don't have to take a trip to the Tools menu to do it, either).

An example: I'm always misspelling, um, *misspell*. I always use one *s* instead of two. When that happens, Word magically corrects it. And how does it know? The easiest way is to show you.

Type **mispell** (spelled wrong, just as you see it here). See the red squiggly line on the screen under that misspelled word (meaning that you've spelled it wrong)? When you're working in Word, and you see that red line, right-click the word, and on the shortcut menu, point to AutoCorrect, and point to the correct spelling. From that moment on, you'll never know you misspelled the word because it's become an AutoCorrect entry—your very own personal AutoCorrect entry. You can do this with any word, any phrase, anything you type at all.

---

**Note**  This feature might embolden the bad spellers of the world, and so I do have mixed feelings about it (although, as I said, this is one of my favorite Office features). I mean, it does tend to make you a lazy speller, at the very least. But this is a wonderful way to free you up a bit so that you aren't constantly fixing typos and misspellings and can spend more time on the real heart of the matter. So use it carefully—look at how the word is spelled after it's been fixed. It just might make you a better speller.

---

# Change Is Good

I could go on and on about the ways you can customize Office so that you're focusing on your work rather than the software. But frankly, you didn't buy this book only to discover pages and pages of procedures. I work with some very talented, smart, and insightful people—people to whom I really should have dedicated this book—who have written scads of information about how to customize just about anything you do in Office. In addition, you'll find hundreds of templates available to you on the Microsoft Office Online Web site (office.microsoft.com—click Templates when you get there) so that you don't have to do any customizing at all if you don't want to—it's all done for you. Also, if you're a regular Crabby Office Lady column reader, you know that I often add tips about how to make you more efficient, making your work life easier and therefore your daily life more enjoyable.

The point is, Office is a tool. And as with any tool, there is a ramp-up time, time spent getting to know the tool, its parts, and the aspects of it that you really need. I encourage you to spend some time customizing your Office programs so that you can use Office the way it's meant to be used: your way.

Think of your Microsoft Office programs as your toolbox: learn how to use your tools, arrange them in a way that makes sense, and please, use protective eyewear if necessary.

Chapter Four
# Surviving Life in the Office

*The gem cannot be polished without friction, nor man perfected without trials.*

— *Chinese proverb*

If you work in an office, you deal with—probably on a daily basis—traffic on the way to work, brash coworkers, lunches stolen from the refrigerator, strenuous collaboration, boredom...and traffic on the way home. While I can't really help you with the traffic issue, I can encourage you to think about the impact you have on others at work. And if you pass this book on to them, perhaps they'll do the same, and then, yes, I will have solved all the known workplace issues. And then there will be Oprah appearances and possibly even a nod from Dr. Phil.

# Etiquette Guide for Working Ladies and Gentlemen

You and I both know that there is more to workplace etiquette than just e-mail manners (although, as you already know, that's a good start). Of course, because I am the Crabby Office Lady, you might think—solely by my moniker—that the quest for perfect manners is not my specialty. And to be honest, it's not. (My greatest talents lie elsewhere. My qualifications lean more toward teaching you to make the best of the Microsoft Office tools that you have at your disposal.) But both you and I might want to consider cleaning up our act a bit at work and starting to cultivate a better overall image for ourselves. (Well, you might, anyway—I make my living cultivating a different sort of attitude.)

So let's give this general workplace courtesy thing a go and see if anything sticks.

## Gossip: Remember the Wounds of Junior High

Get folks together, and gossip will happen. Perhaps it's just part of our nature, or perhaps, it makes some folks feel better about themselves to talk smack about other folks.

Gossiping at work, especially about your coworkers, is destined to come back and bite you in the you-know-what. If you must gossip, be discreet. Better yet, if you can, avoid gossiping.

If you're going to talk about someone, you need to realize that the chances of your words getting back to that person are good (and gossip often finds a way to come back to bite you at a most inopportune time). Consider this example: You repeat a rumor you've heard about Erika to Yvonne; Yvonne repeats it to Stan; Stan makes a beeline for Steve's office; Steve, who's been looking for just the right opportunity to get on Erika's good side, spills it. And Erika (being the resourceful schemer she is) finds out, in about two minutes, who set this unsubstantiated (but completely true) rumor free: you.

Some of us believe that, as human beings, we do have free will and can make the choice not to be sneaky and mean at work. So let me make this short and sweet: don't gossip. It makes both the person you're talking about and you look bad.

## Meetings: Not Every Corner Is a Conference Room

There are meetings and there are meetings. Some are formal meetings that involve an e-mail invitation, an agenda, and a taker of the minutes. And then there are the "nonmeetingish" meetings when you run into someone in the hallway, the restroom, or the cafeteria.

Listen, I know that hallway meetings can be useful and, by their very nature, inescapable. In fact, some hallway meetings can be downright fruitful: short and to the point. But please, if you have something to discuss that is sensitive or personal, take it to an office or a conference room with a closed door—hallways are for walking. If you're getting into a discussion that might require more than a couple of minutes or inspire emphatic waving of hands (and the accompanying danger to passersby), make your way to a less-trafficked spot. Also, don't force innocent folks heading down the hallways into a game of London Bridge, making them walk between you two. Move off to the side and let them pass.

## Stealing Has a Broad Definition

Seems obvious, doesn't it? But I'm not talking about breaking into someone's house or shoplifting one of those ultra-personal items (things that you can't imagine ferrying to the checkout line). Just to set the record straight, the following acts can be considered stealing in the workplace:

- When you park in the handicapped parking space, you're stealing a space from someone who really needs it.

- When you take home a ream of paper, a box of pens, or a couple of those new chairs from the lobby, you're stealing from the very company that already pays you, even if you believe that pay is less than fair.

- When you pad your travel expense report, you're not only stealing, you're lying.

- When you take credit for work done by others, you're stealing their thunder (and possibly altering the outcome of their performance reviews). If you decided to delegate part of a certain project, note exactly who it was who was responsible for completing that part.

You get the idea. If it feels wrong, it probably is. If it feels right, but with a sneaky, I'm-getting-away-with-it vibe, it's also probably wrong.

## Telephone, Telephone, Can You Hear Me?

Ah, yes, the standard communication tool in every office is still the telephone. And while cell phones, instant messaging, and e-mail have encouraged us to loosen our ties or toss out the pantyhose when it comes to non-face-to-face communication, there are still some courtesies worth keeping.

- Answer your phone nicely. Identify who you are. "Um...yello...?" is just not an appropriate way to answer the phone at work.

- If you have to put someone on hold, ask first. Don't just say, "Hold, please," and shut them off. "Please" is not a get-out-of-jail-free card (even my preschool-aged daughter knows that). That being said, I do realize that some of you reading this might work at a busy switchboard and can't coddle and sweet-talk every Tom, Dick, or "do-you-have-Prince-Albert-in-a-can" jokester who calls up. But you get my point.

- If you have an office with a door, close the door if you're going to have a conversation that is long and/or personal. We all have a lot of things to do (and hearing only one side of your conversation is always maddeningly intriguing).

## Cell Phone Etiquette

Yakking on your cell phone to your sweetie-pie in the hallway or bathroom is simply not appropriate, polite, or even cool. Close your office door, go outside, or call from the parking garage (if you can get reception there, that is).

- If we can, let's avoid having a long, private conversation on speakerphone. When I'm trying to be personal and private (and *private* is the key word here) and you're broadcasting our conversation to the world, that tells me something about the level of trust between us.

- When you're in the process of leaving a voice mail, don't be reading your e-mail, applying your makeup, or trying to catch the attention of someone passing by your office. (You're not as good at multitasking as you think you are. Do you really want recorded proof of that?)

I have my own list of serious cell phone pet peeves, but that's a chapter of a different color...

## Communal Spaces: Just Part of Office Life

Unless you're a full-time telecommuter, you probably share some measure of space with other people in your office. This could mean an office, restroom, kitchen, cafeteria, copy room, conference room, or all of the above. So please consider abiding by the following rules:

- Don't take the last cup of coffee without making more.

- Never say anything—out loud, in an instant message, or in e-mail—that you wouldn't want someone else to know. "Privacy" just isn't what it used to be. Not a nice fact, but a fact, nonetheless.

- Related to the preceding item, if you're sharing an office, keep your private conversations with Pookie to a minimum. There's no need to gross-out your officemate.

- Regarding bathroom conversations, you never know who is in the stall next to you or how your voice echoes into adjacent offices (not to mention the other gender's bathroom).

## Socializing: A Little Can Go a Long Way

When I asked a cohort of mine about his views on socializing with coworkers, he told me a long-winded story that involved a business trip, a casino, a hotel room, and a *whole* lot of explaining to do when he got home. While I'll spare you the details here, believe me when I tell you these three things:

- Even if your coworkers have their ties loosened and their hair unpinned, this doesn't mean that you are all free to act as though you are taking part in a fraternity hazing ritual. You are still representing the company you work for (as are your coworkers).

- Watch the alcohol consumption (see the preceding section about gossip).

- Be true to the expense report (see the abbreviated naughty story above and also the section about stealing).

Look, I'm not telling you not to have a good time. But these are not your pals; these are people you work with. And while it can be quite refreshing to see the Crabby Office Lady let loose a bit, this doesn't mean you can just say—or do—anything you want to her. She has a direct line to Human Resources and will have your hungover rear end on the street and looking for work by 8 A.M. Monday.

## Watch Your Language

Yes, we've all had both the urge and the opportunity to use words that would make the longshoremen on the wharves of the Puget Sound blush. However, consider this to be a subset of the "socializing" guideline stated earlier: just because you're feeling a little free, frustrated, or freaked out doesn't mean that you have the right to spew curse words, epithets, or other antisocial language at work.

Even if you're tempted to do this around people you've worked with for years and years, try to hold back. You'll risk embarrassing both yourself and them, and you might even develop a reputation as a <gasp> potty-mouth.

## Instant Messaging, Instant Annoyance

Ah, instant messages: the blessing and the curse of our modern age. While this technology can really speed up communication between team members, it can also be a constant source of nonstop, pop-up irritation.

Instant messaging has its time and place. If you're using it at work as one of your principal ways of communicating, make sure everyone on your team is on board with this type of this technology.

If you and your coworkers are going to make use of instant messaging, or IMing, on a regular basis, be sure to set some ground rules first.

- Do you say "Hi, are you there?" before launching into the message, or do you just launch right into the reason you're IMing in the first place? I asked some coworkers about this and received mixed opinions. One person I talked to suggested saying "hi" before launching into whatever it is that can't wait. Another suggested just the opposite: IMing indicates "instant," so don't waste her time with a greeting. Just get to the point and that's that. I can see both points of view, actually. I guess it just depends on your working style and how you use IM.

- Save sensitive conversations for face-to-face meetings. As I stated in my e-mail etiquette chapter, humans have *emotions*, not *emoticons*.

Again, instant messaging can be quite useful and efficient, but unless you set some boundaries, you might spend your days hopping between 10 different message windows and deciphering cutesy emoticons.

## Dress Code

As I'm sure you've heard by now, generally speaking, the dress code for Microsoft employees is very relaxed. The only reason someone around here is wearing a suit is because he or she is here for an interview, or, um..., there is no other reason.

However, even if you're lucky enough to work in an informal office, this doesn't mean that we (as in you) have free rein to come to work in ratty cut-off shorts and stinky sweat socks. Between you and me, I've even seen more of my coworkers' bare feet and corns than is necessary (or even right).

When I went out into the working world for the first time, my mom and dad always told me to dress for success. And although at that point in history, *success* to my parents meant pantyhose and bunion-producing shoes, this basic tenet still holds true: if you want to be taken seriously, dress the part. I can't offer a specific way to dress if your company is all about being casual, but let me cast my net wide here:

- Wear shoes.
- Take showers regularly.
- Save the bare midriff for the beach or the weekend.
- Don't wear anything that is ripped, torn, or in any way "distressed."

Now that we have a basic idea of how to act in the workplace, it's time to tackle the issue of working with people who might not be so well-behaved.

# How to Work with Difficult People

*Collaboration* is one of the hot terms that we use (and possibly overuse) these days in the workplace. The days of looking out only for yourself have passed, and that is generally a good thing, because sharing the burden means sharing the success. But as you know, the workplace draws all sorts of personalities, and in fact, some folks can be torture to work with, even though they can be downright great at what they do. So how do you collaborate with them and still keep your sanity? For starters, you can let Microsoft Office be the go-between.

## SharePoint: Sharing from Afar

Say it out loud with me: Microsoft Windows SharePoint Services. (The name itself just screams collaboration, doesn't it?)

A SharePoint site is basically a Web site that someone—or some team—in your company sets up where you and your coworkers can work together on a single project or a series of projects. You can post announcements and pictures, have discussions, share links,

### When Difficult People Make Your Work Even More Difficult

You can avoid face-to-face contact with those people with whom you *must* work but who make your blood pressure rise and your manners dash out the back door. Take a look at what SharePoint, OneNote, and Live Meeting can offer with regard to working together...in separate corners. Virtual workspaces and meetings, as well as shared note-taking sessions, shouldn't be an everyday substitute for meeting people eye-to-eye, but they're great tools for when you can't (or just can't stand to) meet with someone in person.

upload and work on documents, and coordinate schedules. A SharePoint site is pretty unlimited, really—it all depends on what you want to do and how you want to do it.

In our case, we want to squeeze as much work as possible out of our difficult coworkers with the least amount of distress. And while a SharePoint site has scads of features that will allow you to do this, I picked two features to highlight, ones that seem specifically designed for collaboration-from-afar. Once you are familiar with your own SharePoint site, you might come up with even more ways to keep a working relationship alive and well while avoiding being cast in others' workplace soap operas.

## Meeting Workspaces: Get Together Without Getting Together

A meeting workspace is a type of SharePoint Web site that acts as a central spot to house all the information you need for those non-face-to-face meetings you'll be having with Ms. Persnickety. There you can publish agendas, documents you plan to discuss, meeting notes, results, and so on. It's like a repository for every meeting and its results (or lack thereof). When you send a meeting request to little Ms. P, include a hyperlink that goes to the workspace, where she can learn about the meeting details and whatnot.

## Document Workspaces: Virtual Collaboration

A document workspace is another type of SharePoint site, but instead of keeping track of meeting information, it's a virtual (read: imaginary and yet somehow real) place where you and Mr. Negativity (Ms. P's officemate, which might explain things a bit...) can collaborate on presentations, documents, spreadsheets, and drawings. The neat thing about document workspaces is that you can choose how you want to collaborate.

- Send Mr. N a shared attachment via e-mail. You just create a new piece of mail in Microsoft Office Outlook, add the document as an attachment, and work with the settings in the Attachment Options task pane.

- Use the Create button in the Shared Workspace task pane to create a document workspace in Word, Excel, PowerPoint, or Visio. Then add the names of the people who have access to the files and decide whether you want to send them an invitation. (I suggest that you do this unless you want to call them or meet them face-to-face—and that's kind of what we're trying to avoid, right?)

- Create a private document workspace for a document that is already published in a document library on your SharePoint site.

- Create a document workspace site in a Web browser.

So instead of having to send versions of the files back and forth through e-mail or even <oh, no, not again> meet to discuss the project, you've made Mr. N an automatic workspace member. This means that he can work on the files on his own computer, and by using the Shared Workspace task pane, he can make changes to the files, get updates, and even check off that long list of tasks you've assigned to him. (Who's thinking negative now, mister? Huh?)

The most important aspect of using a document workspace is that all of us always have access to the most recent version of the project we're working on. And we're not even breathing the same air.

Now that you have a meeting workspace set up and a document workspace set up, too, you're all set to collaborate, plan, schedule, and interact with one another quite effectively and without one of you ever losing your temper, your manners, or your mind. How's that for customer satisfaction?

For more information about Windows SharePoint Services technology, visit Office Online at office.microsoft.com.

# Use OneNote for Sharing Your Notes

If your company isn't on board with SharePoint (the nerve!), or if you want to try something else, consider OneNote, Microsoft's note-taking program. OneNote offers a variety of ways to share notes with others and collaborate in absentia.

- Send notes in an e-mail message (whether or not your grumpy recipient has OneNote).

- Publish or move your notes to a shared location, such a network share.

- Start (or end) a shared note-taking session.

This last one is my favorite. By using the Shared Session feature in OneNote, you can all take part in a peer-to-peer note-taking session, interacting and working with your ideas on shared OneNote pages. As long as everyone is on the same network, you can all work on the same notes whether you're in one room together, holed up in your individual cubicles, or even working from home.

Sounds like magic, doesn't it? Well, in a way it is, and when I first tried it out, I pestered everyone I knew with it. You can literally hold live, one-to-many note-taking or brainstorming sessions, each from the comfort of your own office. Here's how it works: I invite you to a session, you join in, and there you have it. You stay on your side of the fence, and I stay on mine. But we share our ideas by writing, typing, or drawing.

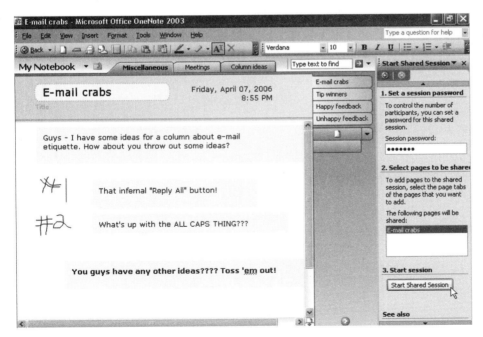

For more information about OneNote share note-taking sessions, visit go.microsoft.com/fwlink/?LinkId=61477.

## Live Meeting: Your Interactive Web Conferencing Service

Microsoft Office Live Meeting is a Web conferencing technology that lets you hold meetings with large or small groups of people from all over the planet. All you need is a phone, a personal computer with an Internet connection, and a browser. It's real-time collaboration without the real-time aggravation! What could be better? Here's what you can do with Live Meeting:

- Use interactive tools such as the electronic whiteboard to mark up files, create flowcharts, and more. Meeting attendees can see exactly what you're doing—including your mouse movements and what you're doing on your keyboard (a little overkill, if you ask me). You can also share only a portion of your screen to keep your audience focused on the key information (now that's more my style).

- Take your audience to live Web pages. Each meeting attendee can click on links, fill out forms, or use interactive media. And here's when this feature really comes into its own: You know when you mistype something in the Address bar in your browser and end up on a site that is, shall we say, not G-rated? This feature allows you to see the page before you show it to other meeting attendees.

- Save your meeting content and give your participants the ability to print the content. Or record the meeting with the audio and visuals synchronized so that everyone can access the information they need—even after the meeting has ended.

- Travel less. Why walk across the hall when you can pull down the shades, close your door, and get your ideas across without all that hair rending and silent cursing? And if your difficult coworker lives in Italy, all the better.

    Of course, Live Meeting *really* starts to pay for itself when you're dealing with people who aren't just down the hall. Can you imagine your savings on airfare, time spent in security lines at the airport, and that hotel minibar bill?

For more information, visit the Live Meeting home page at go.microsoft.com/fwlink /?LinkId=35524.

# Final Words on Avoiding Your Coworkers and Clients

Some of you may be completely aghast that I've gone on ad nauseum about how to collaborate with coworkers without ever having to see them. Of course I don't want you to do this 100 percent of the time. It's not good to run from the challenges that face you in your life. Think about Tony Soprano: He has that fight/flight thing going on. Whenever he has to confront something uncomfortable in his life, he has a panic attack. But even Tony is working on that, right? Maybe you should, too.

So listen. Sometimes it's better to try and work with prickly coworkers in a personal manner, but sometimes you need to do the best you can with the tools you've got. And that's the point: collaboration—which you might think includes only a whiteboard and fancy markers and being broken up into groups with people you have nothing in common with—does not have to mean being forced into a windowless room with folks who raise our blood pressure and lower our expectations. Do the right thing, won't you?

Getting along with everyone all the time isn't easy (for most of us, anyway). Sometimes it's better to just suck it up, walk down the hall, and talk to that thorn in your side. Go ahead: take the high road.

# Tackling Big Projects and Still Keeping Your Wits About You

Finally. You've finally managed to get a handle on your daily workload and tie up some loose ends that have been nagging at you forever. Now maybe you can breathe a little easier and get out of the office when you eat lunch (and save your poor keyboard from all that spillage).

But no, someone up the ladder—someone on a rung higher than yours who has the power to press footprints onto your tender scalp—has had yet another 3 A.M. epiphany about yet another big project that is destined to change the way people think about life (or at least the way you think about middle management). And of course, you're the only one who can handle the job. So how do you manage to keep your regular workload under control while tackling this new monster? Repeat after me: *organization* and *delegation*.

## Organization: Start with Your Inbox

You know that being organized is a major part of being successful on the job. (I don't mean that your desk has to be neat and tidy. In fact, there is a famous quote about how a cluttered desk is the sign of a cluttered mind, but I think that's a bunch of hooey.)

In any case, if someone has assigned you a new, gargantuan project, keeping track of your regular job duties as well as this new one takes some doing. Outlook Search Folders and flags are my way of tackling this issue.

## Search Folders

I'm a big fan of Outlook Search Folders—in fact, I use them constantly. A Search Folder in Outlook works like an Internet search, but it searches your mailbox instead of the Internet, and it searches all the time. The results of the search appear in the Search Folder and are, in essence, links to things you keep in other folders. In other words, the Search Folder is a virtual folder; you don't actually move or drag things to it.

Outlook 2003, and later, includes three default Search Folders: For Follow Up, Large Mail, and Unread Mail. Any item with a flag appears in the For Follow Up folder; any item larger than 100 KB appears in the Large Mail folder; and any mail you haven't read yet appears in the Unread Mail folder (and if it's larger than 100 KB, it appears in that Large Mail folder, too). But let me repeat: these messages aren't actually in those Search Folders; they contain only shortcuts that you have this kind of mail.

Of course, you can customize the Search Folders to contain and search for almost anything you want. For example, let's take that big, looming project. You create a Search Folder so that whenever an e-mail message from so-and-so containing a phrase that is related to this new project (such as *marketing juju*) comes barreling through the bandwidth, a link to it gets tossed into the Search Folder you set up to find messages with that criteria. That way, you don't have to go through all your e-mail messages to figure out which ones pertain to the new project and which ones are parts of your daily work.

Suppose you don't want (or can't use) the three default Search Folders—Follow Up, Large Mail, and Unread Mail—in Outlook. Never fear; you can create your own.

1. In **Mail**, on the **File** menu, click the **New** drop-down arrow, and then click **Search Folder**.
2. Click **Create a custom Search Folder**.
3. Under **Customize Search Folder**, click **Choose**.
4. Type a name for your custom Search Folder.
5. Click **Criteria**, select the options you want, and then click **OK**.
6. Click **Browse**, select the folders that you want the search criteria to search, and then click **OK** three times.

Now, if you do like the *ideas* of the default folders given to you, but you don't exactly agree with the *criteria* assigned to them, you can change that, too.

1. In **Mail**, on the **File** menu, click the **New** drop-down arrow, and then click **Search Folder**.
2. Click a predefined Search Folder.

3. If prompted, under **Customize Search Folder**, specify the criteria to use.

4. To select a different mailbox to search, under **Customize Search Folder**, click the drop-down arrow, and then select a mailbox from the list.

---

**Note**  When you delete a Search Folder, the messages shown in the Search Folder are not deleted, because those items are never *saved*, only *viewed*, in a Search Folder. However, if you open or select one or more e-mail messages shown in a Search Folder and delete the e-mail messages, the messages will be deleted from the Outlook folder where they are stored. In words, vanish from the folder they really lived in as well as their vacation homes, their assigned Search Folders.

---

## Flags

I love flags. And I don't mean the kind that wave atop a flagpole or are raised above the medal winners at the Olympic Games. Nope, I mean follow-up flags. Briefly, once an e-mail message comes in, you can attach a follow-up flag to it, and a copy of that message will be popped into the Follow Up folder. You just right-click the message, point to Follow Up, and select the flag color you want to assign to it.

---

**Note**  If you've kept the default For Follow Up Search Folder, your flagged messages show up in that Search Folder as well as in the Follow Up folder (they aren't the same thing). If you ask me, there's no need to have both—why waste a perfectly good Search Folder? This would be a great time to consider creating a Search Folder of your own.

---

Certain messages weigh more heavily—on your mind, on your conscience, on your schedule, whatever—than others. You can keep the default names for these flags (Red Flag, Blue Flag, Yellow Flag—gee, aren't those unique), or you can customize them to fit your needs. You can also pick colors, assign text to the flags, and specify whether you want to show just the colored flag next to the message, just the text, or both the text and the colored flag.

What I do is name my flags according to when I need to follow up on that particular message: Next Week, Right Away, When-The-Hot-Place-Below-Freezes-Over, and so on. Once you've accomplished whatever the message indicated that you needed to do, you can unflag that baby and consider it done. So take some time on the Office Online Web site to figure out how you can customize your flags. Then wave them proudly.

## Delegation: Share the Love (and the Work)

A little delegation goes a long way when you need to get something done, and as we all know, everyone has different talents. It's time to leverage those endowments we all have.

- If you're all working on the same network, give the people helping you on this project sharing permissions on your private folders. You can choose which folders you want to make accessible and how much control each person is granted (author, editor, reader, and so on). You can do this with SharePoint, too.

- Set up delegate access permissions in Outlook. This means that you can have your delegates send messages and accept meeting and task requests for you, and even manage information in your private Outlook folders. And just as with private folders, you control how much access you want to grant to your Outlook account.

---

For more information about how to give others access to your private folders, read the assistance article "Permit Others to Access Folders" at go.microsoft.com /fwlink/?LinkId=63208. Note that you all have to be using Outlook with Exchange Server to use this feature.

---

- Assign tasks in Outlook with specific start and end dates. Then ask your delegates to follow up when they've completed parts of the project you've assigned to them.

---

For more information about how (and even why) to set up delegate access permissions, take the free online training course titled "Delegate Access Basics," available at go.microsoft.com/fwlink/?LinkId=63207

---

Chapter 6, "Making the Most of Performance Reviews," goes into more detail about delegation for managers. But even if you're not a manager, sharing the burden can make a huge project seem less forbidding. But remember: don't just share the work—share the credit, too.

# Everyone Has It: Dealing with Boredom at Work

Let's face it: sometimes you'd rather be doing something—anything—else than sitting at your desk slaving away at a spreadsheet or concocting yet another presentation that will induce much yawning and grocery list writing. I want to offer you 10 ways to ease your boredom while still being (arguably) productive by using all that your brain and Office have to offer.

But if you think I'm going to advise you about how to waste time at work, think again, sweetie. I want you to be productive while you're bored at work so that you're not really wasting time. (OK, I admit it—this last bit has been gratuitously added here for you managers who believe that all your direct reports are hard at work and happy about it.)

I do understand that there are times when you might not feel like making one more cold call to one more cold person, reading one more souped-up résumé, or squeezing out one more grant proposal. When I hit one of those spots and my mind starts to turn to mush, I breathe in, breathe out, click my heels three times, and start to play around with some of the Office tools at my disposal. (Frankly, it's how I get a lot of my column ideas.)

## Idea #1: Perk Up Your Documents with Clip Art

No, this doesn't have to be gratuitous clip art that overwhelms the content of your message. But a little visual impact can make the difference between a dry <cough> document that encourages naptime and one that keeps your readers' eyes open and sparkly (go.microsoft.com/fwlink/?LinkId=9479).

## Idea #2: Download Templates for Vacation Planning

A smart company knows that happy, rested people are productive people. So whether you're planning to rough it with a backpack or wrap yourself in luxury at every four-star resort on our little blue planet, start planning your trip now. (Or make it a last-minute thing and risk spending the July 4th holiday weekend tent-to-tent with strangers in a crowded public campsite.) (go.microsoft.com/fwlink/?LinkId=60514)

## Idea #3: Read a Crabby Column

Yes, this can be educational and fun at the same time (or so I'm told). (go.microsoft.com/fwlink/?LinkId=61380)

---

### Crabby Office Lady
Assistance

**Solid advice with an attitude**

Here's a list of the columns I've cranked out so far. If you haven't read them, please do so now. You never know when you'll be quizzed on the topics I'll be featuring.

Think Crabby isn't real? View her live action videos and see for yourself. While you're at it, take a look at our Office demos that are guaranteed to make you a better Office user.

- The Crabby Office Lady video archive
- Get Crabby's columns via RSS
- Office Demos Showcase

---

## Idea #4: Set Up Outlook to Get Your Personal Mail, Too

If the hardworking Outlook team goes to the trouble of allowing you to create multiple e-mail accounts so that you can wage all your spam wars on one battlefield, you owe it to them to do just that.

One caveat: make sure you're sending work mail from your work account. You wouldn't want your manager getting your weekly status mail from your personal mail account, would you, TwinkleToes@yourdomain.com?

## Idea #5: Use Speech Recognition and Never Be Lonely Again

Do you tire of typing but never of hearing the sound of your own voice? Then speech recognition is for you. With the proper setup, you can dictate text into any Office program and select menus, toolbars, and dialog boxes by using your voice. It's fun, it's easy, and it makes a great party trick.

## Idea #6: Practice Your PowerPoint Techniques

Yes, in theory, you can use every possible PowerPoint animation and page transition available, but you don't want your presentation to be confused with a video game or make your audience queasy. I suggest you try out everything—the animations, the transitions, the color schemes, the various templates—and then figure out what works best for your content, your audience, and the point you're trying to make.

## Idea #7: Create a New E-Mail Signature

Yes, you can make your signature outrageously long, complicated, and with more information than the message itself. And yes, that can be funny...once. Your e-mail signature can be as simple as your name, or a *Thanks*, or even a *Thanks* with your name and your home page Web address in there, too.

## Idea #8: Frolic in the Research Task Pane

Learn obscure facts from the Microsoft Encarta encyclopedia about everyone and everything from Abba Eban to Zulu bow music. Or translate a note into Chinese that you've written to your pen pal in Beijing. Or get real-time stock quotes, look up words in the Microsoft Encarta dictionary, or become a better writer with the thesaurus.

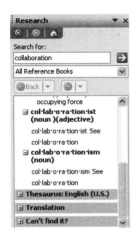

# Idea #9: Learn Your Keyboard Shortcuts

You don't know what a keyboard shortcut is? Well, try this (and then get right back here!): You know that little button with the Windows icon on the lower left and lower right of your keyboard between the CTRL and ALT keys? It's called the Windows logo key. (Crazy, isn't it?) Press Windows+M and see what happens... Don't worry, you can click the taskbar buttons to reopen all the windows that suddenly shut.

Fun, eh? As you may have figured out, keyboard shortcuts are a way to accomplish tasks quickly—sometimes more quickly than using your mouse. And if you can't use (or don't want to use) a mouse, keyboard shortcuts are your main way of accessing and doing just about anything.

---

**Tip**   To find out what the keyboard shortcuts are for the program you're working in, press F1, and then type **keyboard shortcuts** in the Search box. Note that you can also create your own keyboard shortcuts that correspond to the tasks you do most often.

---

# Idea #10: Consider a Career Change

If you're bored at work, perhaps it's time to change jobs. Now, I'm not saying that you should do your job searching while you're at your current job. (I can already hear the e-mail messages from your managers careening through the Internet pipeline on their way to me.) But you can use the Office Online tools to jump-start your career. There you'll find résumé and cover letter templates, as well as job search letters and tools.

Now you have no excuse to be bored (or get caught trolling Web sites you shouldn't be trolling). There is plenty out there (and in here) to do. It's just a matter of finding it. You might even have fun while you're at work. Imagine that.

## You're Not Just Surviving—You're Thriving

Now you have a few tips on how to deal with the trials and tribulations of office life. I understand that it's not always easy to deal with coworkers' bad manners and abrasive working styles, seemingly random big projects assigned to you, and boredom. But I have one last tip to offer: keep it all in perspective. Yes, this is your job, and its paycheck allows you to live a certain lifestyle to which you aspire. But if you can keep your wits (and your manners) about you and use the tools at your disposal (namely, some of the Office tools described in this chapter), you can make your daily toil a little less laborious and a whole lot more enjoyable.

Chapter Five

# Managing People, Projects,...and Yourself

*No person will make a great business who wants to do it all himself or get all the credit.*

— *Andrew Carnegie*

Being a manager is not an easy job. Come to think of it, neither is being managed. Both require a certain modicum of respect for the people you work for and you work with, as well as for yourself. If you don't think you're doing a great job, how can the people below and above you (on that infamous ladder) believe it?

Whether you're the manager or someone being managed, you're required to carry out any number of tasks throughout the workday (in addition to those important looming projects and your basic daily workload). There are a number of steps you can take to make those daily responsibilities and duties run a bit smoother, thereby making your workday feel a bit less oppressive. And so this chapter covers three of the things that I find help make this happen (for both managers and nonmanagers): being an effective meeting leader, sharing your workload (also known as *delegating*), and making sure those private documents you're sending to a public printer remain private until you're ready to share them.

# How to Prepare For and Run Effective Meetings

Calling, attending, and leading meetings are some of those less-than-thrilling chores that almost everyone who works in an office is required to fulfill. If you're the one calling the meeting, being prepared, which could mean inviting the right people and keeping the conversation on track, can ensure that the meeting is fruitful and not a waste of your—not to mention your attendees'—time.

So you need to get everyone together for a meeting. Maybe it's a recurring meeting; maybe it's a one-time thing. As you probably already know, calling a meeting is just the first step to actually making it a successful one. Once everyone is gathered and looking at you expectantly, it's your job to make the most of their time and yours. But it's your meeting, and you have every right to run it how you please, right? Yes, but since this is the workplace, a point where personalities of all varieties come together, meeting leaders have their own particular (even peculiar) ways of doing things.

**The headmistress**    Stands at the head of the table with her arms crossed and silently waits until all eyes are on her before calling the meeting to order. This is a great technique for keeping order and scaring your attendees; it's lousy if collaboration and brainstorming are part of the plan.

**The freewheeler**    Lets everyone shout out their ideas, go out for snacks, talk amongst themselves, and make paper airplanes out of the handouts. Fun times? Heck yeah, dude! Organized and productive times? Not so much.

**The stickler**    Keeps a copy of Robert's Rules of Order on hand and makes sure there are no infractions. Orderly? Of course. Successful? It depends on what your idea of "successful" is. If your attendees are afraid to speak out of order, silence will be, shall we say, less than golden.

Whatever type you are, you could probably benefit from a quick overview of some guidelines to help you get the most from your meetings. I've outlined five steps to create and run a successful meeting as well as what to do with the results that come from it. Let's get to it.

# Step 1: What's the Purpose of the Meeting?

OK, so, what's the best way to get to Carnegie Hall? Practice, practice, practice. And what's one of the best ways to ensure a successful meeting (on your part, anyway)? Plan, plan, plan.

Creating a meeting agenda that gives an overview of the points you want to discuss is a great way to make sure that you don't show up unprepared. And, by golly, Office Online provides templates for just that very thing—the "agenda" thing, not the "unprepared" thing. (One doesn't need a template for that unless one has some sort of over-preparation disability, but that's a topic for a different sort of book with a different sort of author.)

1. Go to the Office Online Templates Web site (go.microsoft.com/fwlink /?LinkId=60514), and type **meeting agenda**. You'll find more than 100 templates, ranging from Formal Meeting Agenda to Informal Meeting Agenda and from Meeting Minutes to Meeting Agenda. What we're looking for here are agendas.

2. Pick one, download it, and customize it. You'll feel prepared, and the folks at your meeting will understand that you mean business.

I suggest that you send this agenda to every person you want to invite to this meeting and include it in the meeting request in Microsoft Office Outlook (either as an attachment or as text). You also need to figure out whether you'll need audio or visual aids (a projector, handouts, and so on) and, of course, your snack plan. Snacks can be good motivators that magically transform invitees into participants. My mother (or was it my manager?) once told me, "The best way to your employees' free hour between 3 P.M. and 4 P.M. is through their stomachs" (or something like that).

Now that you have your game plan, you'll need to get everyone you need in the same room together. (If you're using Microsoft Office Live Meeting because you're working with folks from all over the globe or you're just a misanthrope, you'll still have to get them into the same *virtual* room together.)

# Step 2: Call That Meeting!

The most efficient way I know to send out a meeting request is to use Microsoft Office Outlook. (Since I'm the Crabby *Office* Lady, this shouldn't come as any surprise to you.) You've probably done this a zillion times and maybe you're an old pro, but let's review. Here is what I believe to be the easiest way to send out a meeting request:

1. If you're using Outlook 2003 (and I must assume you are), in **Calendar**, on the **Actions** menu, click **Plan a Meeting**.

2. Click **Add Others**, and then click **Add from Address Book**.

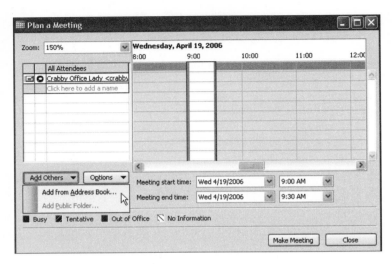

3. In the **Type name or select from list** box, enter the name of a person or resource you want at the meeting.

4. When you find the name of the person you want to invite, select his or her name in the list, and then click the **Required** or **Optional** button. (The **Required** and **Optional** attendees appear in the **To** box on the **Appointment** tab.) If you want to schedule a conference room, locate it in the Address Book, and then add it to the **Resources** box. Click **OK**.

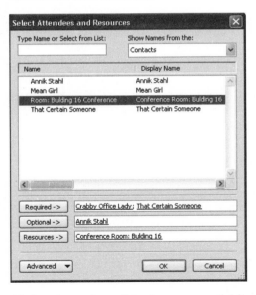

5. Click a time when all invitees are available. (You can use **AutoPick Next** to find the next available free time for all invitees.)

6.  Click **Make Meeting**.

7.  In the **Subject** box, type a description for the meeting. Be specific. **Meeting with Crabby** could be just about anything (and, frankly, usually is).

---

**Tip**  If you did not schedule a room (by adding it, in step 4, to the **Resources** box), type the location in the **Location** box.

---

8.  If you want to make the meeting recurring, click **Recurrence**, and then select the recurrence pattern.

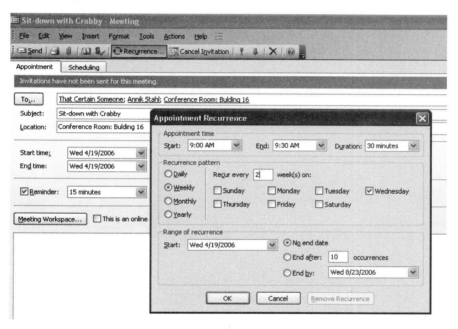

9.  Select any other options you want.

10. Click **Send**.

Be sure to add your agenda by clicking File on the Insert menu and selecting the agenda document. Alternatively, you can add the agenda as text to the body of the meeting. And if your meeting is one of a series of meetings or if there is a lot of planning on both your part and your attendees' parts, perhaps creating a Meeting Workspace (which requires Outlook 2003) is the way to go. That way you can have a centralized place for people to collaborate on a project and have a record of what was decided in a meeting.

OK, you've sent out the meeting request...and now the real work begins.

# Step 3: Sign 'em In and Keep Track of What's Going On

OK. Everyone is here, enjoying the snacks, and going over the agenda that you so efficiently sent out with the meeting request. (Aren't you on top of things!) Let's get this party started!

First, how about having everyone sign in so that we can berate those who didn't show up? Head on back to the Office Online Templates Web site, and download and print a meeting sign-in sheet.

---

**Note** Between you and me, it's a lot easier (and less unsightly) to give you real text to type in the Search box instead of lengthy URLs that you're likely to mistype. So from now on, anytime you see a template name in **bold**, that's your cue to type those *exact* words in the Search box on the Office Online Templates Web site (or any site on the Office Online Web site, for that matter).

---

Now that everyone is well fed and signed in, it's time to start the meeting. First you might want to go over what you're going to discuss and perhaps make sure that everyone knows everyone else. Then you can jump right into your presentation, documents, spreadsheets, or whatever else you've brought. But before you do that, let's grab a template that will keep track of everything that's happened in the meeting, otherwise known as the *minutes*.

The time-honored way to keep track of all that's going to go on at your meeting is to have someone take meeting minutes. I like to volunteer the person sitting in front to do it. (Hey, if he's going to show up early and play teacher's pet, he has it coming.)

And, no surprise, we have a template for meeting minutes, too. Head on over to the Office Online Templates Web site, type **minutes**, and download a template that suits your particular sensibilities. (There are too many templates to list here.) Next up: meeting preparation.

# Step 4: Prepare Your Documents

If you've decided to call a meeting, you'd better have a good reason for it. People are very, very busy these days, and they have no compunction about telling you so. If you show up with well-structured spreadsheets, compelling presentations, and persuasive documents (in handout form, of course) that just may save the free world from, say, the scourge of bad e-mail etiquette, your attendees will have no choice but to sit up in their chairs, transfixed and more alive than they've ever been before. (OK, that's taking it a little far, but I like outrageous yet attainable goals—you can encourage your attendees to go for the same, through example.)

I suggest you mosey on over to the Office Online Web site and take a gander at what it takes to make a meeting fruitful: coherent and meaningful spreadsheets, vivacious (yet not overwhelming) Microsoft Office Power-Point presentations, and convincing documents. You'll not only win over your attendees in that particular meeting, you'll have them making sure that the agenda you've set moves forward after the meeting's over.

## Step 5: Action Items!

At the end of the meeting, make sure you talk about what needs to happen next (we like to call these *action items*), and also let your attendees know when and where you'll be posting the results of the meeting. You can either post the meeting notes on a Meeting Workspace or other team Web site or send them through e-mail. That way, everyone will have a point of reference for what you all discussed and decided. This is particularly helpful for those folks who looked like they were taking copious notes but who were actually composing their grocery lists (and you know who you are).

## Navigating the Office Templates Home Page

When you visit this home page, you'll find that you have choices when it comes to locating exactly the template you need. You can browse templates by category (for example, greeting cards, legal documents, or career templates such as resumes and cover letters). And if you already know the program for which you want a template, you can go right to that program (by clicking Microsoft Office Programs under Browse Templates), pick the program you want, and then browse by category from there.

The hard-working Templates team also describes three featured templates, found under the listings Built By Request, Staff Pick, and Featured Template. These featured templates are updated regularly and might be seasonal templates (such as tournament brackets), really popular templates (such as specific PowerPoint design templates), or just those templates that they, as a team who contemplates templates every day, all day, think might be useful (and even fun) for you to know about.

And don't forget, you can also suggest a template if you didn't find what you were looking for. Under the three featured templates is a link that says, "Have a suggestion for a template? Tell us!"

## Final Words About Meetings

As you can see, these five steps highlight basic ways to make sure that your meeting is a success. I know this isn't rocket science, but you'd be surprised how much meeting time you (and others) can waste because of a lack of easy preparation. Every meeting has its own set of special circumstances, so try and come prepared. Chances are, you (not to mention your attendees) will get more out of this approach than if you, say, ran down the hall shouting, "Meeting! Meeting in two minutes! Last one in is a rotten egg!"

If you don't really need to call a meeting, *don't*. We all have a lot to do, and a meeting called just for the heck of it is a waste of everyone's time.

# Delegation: It Doesn't Have to Mean "Passing the Buck"

Handing off some work isn't a sign of weakness; it says that you trust others and need to get rid of the bags under your eyes. I know you're a doer—not just a talker—and everyone else knows that about you, too. You're a multitasking whiz kid, burning the midnight oil, taking the heat when the office burns down, and then putting out the fire. See, I used to be like that, too. But then my family grew, and well, it was a wake-up call to let me know that I didn't need to do all of it all the time all by myself and that I was not only stealing the thunder from my coworkers, I was also woefully underutilizing their considerable talents. So I learned the *D* word: delegation.

## The Path to Delegation Is Paved with Good Intentions

Like anything else you undertake, you can't just jump in there willy-nilly and start delegating everything to everyone. You need to figure out how to get started, what needs delegating, and who is the best person to share what part of the job.

- Figure out why you haven't delegated before. Is it because you don't trust others to do the job? Or is it because you just don't want to take the time to explain what needs to be done?

- Also, figure out what needs delegating. While you're at it, remember that there are some things that you should really keep for yourself (firing someone, writing performance reviews, and volunteering to host a group of six giggly little girls for a sleepover with your daughter are just a few duties best kept for yourself).

- Find the best people for each task, and be sure to communicate exactly what you expect of them: give them lots of information and set specific goals that they can report to you as each task is complete (or semicomplete).

- Let go. Check up when necessary. Give feedback. Let go again.

Now that you have a better idea of why to do what you want to do, we need to figure out just how to use Microsoft Office to make sure that your delegating is successful.

## Share the Information, Share the Love

We're taught early on that sharing is good. And you know, it *is* good. For a lot of reasons. It's good because it relieves you of some of the burden, and it's good because it gives other folks a chance to get their hands dirty, so to speak. Here are a few ways you can share some of your workload by using delegates in Outlook.

Delegating does not mean "passing the buck." Sharing the burden also means sharing the success and can enable a sense of team spirit. Go team!

> **Note**   A majority of the following tips require that you and your delegates are using Outlook in an organization that's running Microsoft Exchange Server.

## I Give You Permission to Help Me

Your private folders (such as your Tasks folder and your Calendar) are, by default, private. But if you want your coworkers or even your manager to be able to see certain things that you're working on, perhaps you should give them permissions to view certain private folders by sharing them. You, as the permissions manager, can specify exactly how extensive these permissions are by setting a person up as a reviewer (someone who can just read the items), as an author (someone who can read and create items, as well as modify and delete items that they themselves create), or as an editor (someone who can do everything an author can do plus modify and delete items you, the manager, created). Here's how you share a public or private folder using permissions:

1. On the **Go** menu, click **Folder List**, right-click the folder you want to share, and then click **Sharing** on the shortcut menu.

2. Click the **Permissions** tab.

3. Click **Add**.

4. In the **Type name or select from list** box, type the name of the person you want to grant sharing permissions to.

5. Click **Add**, and then click **OK**.

6. In the **Name** box, click the name of the person you just added.

7. Under **Permissions**, select the setting you want.

### How to Check Whether You're Using Exchange Server

You can check whether you're using an e-mail account with Exchange Server very quickly (saving you time and aggravation when you're wondering why you can't access some of the features mentioned in this chapter as well as in this book):

1. On the **Tools** menu, click **E-mail Accounts**.

2. Click **View or change existing e-mail accounts**, and then click **Next**.

3. In the **E-mail Accounts** dialog box, your e-mail accounts are listed under **Name**, and the types of account they are (usually POP, HTTP, IMAP, or Exchange) are listed under **Type**.

You might have multiple accounts listed there, and if Exchange is one of them, you're using Exchange Server (meaning that you have access to some of the features I'm talking about in this chapter, such as calendar sharing and setting up delegate access).

## Represent Me, Won't You?

You know what a delegate is, don't you? (Someone to do your bidding, of course.) In this case, a delegate is someone to whom you've given permission to send messages for you, accept meeting and task requests for you, and actually manage information in your private folders. For example, if I send an e-mail message to Bill Gates, I'm pretty much guaranteed that he won't see it until his delegate has taken a good hard look at it first.

## Leave (Almost) Nothing Secret

Make your work an open book. Create a separate folder—a public folder—outside of your own mailbox that other Exchange users in your company can access. These folders are a great way to share information or work on projects together.

You see, these public folders can contain any type of Outlook item, such as messages, appointments, contacts, tasks, journal entries, notes, forms, files, and postings. When you're connected to your Exchange server, folders labeled Public Folders appear in the Outlook Folder List in the Navigation pane.

Now everyone can share Outlook items related to a specific subject or project. You are no longer working in a vacuum.

## A Tisket, a Tasket, Let's Clean Out That Task Basket

Now that you non-Exchange users are thoroughly disgusted with me, I'm going to give you a tip about how to delegate some work when you're not using Exchange Server.

If you're at all like me, you're a list maker. And you probably keep a list of everything you need to do—for work and your personal life—in your Tasks folder. I frankly cannot do without this helpful little friend. I use it to keep track of everything from my daily tasks (read customer e-mail messages and sort the customers from the stalkers) to my personal to-do list (de-flea the Crabby Office Dog).

## Your Options When Turning a Message into a Task

For whatever reason, the options you have when you want to turn a message into a task are not well known. Select the message, hold down the right mouse button, and then drag the message to the Tasks folder in the Navigation pane. Then you get three choices:

**Copy here as a task with text.** The message will stay in the mailbox folder it's in, and the contents of the message, including the subject line and body of the message, will appear in the task.

**Copy here as task with attachment.** A task will be created with the same Subject as the message, but the e-mail message itself is an attachment. The message stays in the folder it's in.

**Move here as task with attachment.** This is similar to the preceding option, but the message is not just an attachment in the task, it is also deleted from its original folder.

Sometimes this list gets a little, shall we say, *bloated*. Then it's time to share the list. If you're a manager, *sharing* is also known as *delegating*. If you're not a manager, *sharing* is sometimes known as *passing the buck*.

- Assign tasks to someone else, and ask them to finish those tasks within a certain time frame. Doing this is simple and painless (for you, anyway), and it'll lighten your load in no time.

- Share your tasks. This means setting up permissions on your Tasks folder so that anyone—or certain people you specify—can access that folder to help you achieve the tasks at hand.

- Turn a message into a task. (I love this one: My manager sends me a message requesting something ridiculous of me, and I turn it into a task for you! So simple and yet so beautiful.)

## A Final Word About Delegating

Don't forget the kudos. Now that you've freed up a little of your time, make sure you take the time to give credit where credit is due. Acknowledge your delegates; you're likely not only to give them more job satisfaction, but you'll also have more willing delegates next time the opportunity to lighten your load comes along.

# Secure Printing: Avoiding That Mad Dash to the Copy Room

We spend a fair amount of time making sure that our computers, our documents, and our private information are kept secure. But all that time and energy can be all for naught if you share a network printer.

You know it, you need it, you use it every day: the copy room. It's the place for ad hoc meetings, copy machine tantrums (its and yours), and petty pen and legal pad theft. It's also a hot spot for confidential information, lying in a pile at the printer, patiently waiting for you (or everyone else) to pick it up.

See, I don't want to see you ever again, clad in business attire, red-faced and panting, galloping frantically across the building toward the copy room to retrieve that confidential document, only to find that someone already gathered it up with everything else. And how can we avoid this unsightly image? By reading this next section, which will teach you how to print securely when you're using a network printer.

# What Is a Network Printer?

If you're sitting at your desk (or standing, as I do), and you can see the umbilical cord connecting a printer to your computer, you're not using a network printer. Your printer is there to do your bidding and no one else's. However (and this is a big however), if you and your coworkers share a printer, one that's available to others in your organization who know how to connect to it, you're in a shared printer environment. And as warm and fuzzy as that sounds, that makes your documents, your spreadsheets, and anything else you're sending to the printer (wherever it's located) vulnerable to prying eyes, whether or not those eyes mean to pry.

Depending on the type of printer you're connected to and how your network is set up, there is usually a way, from within your Office program, to delay printing until you're good and ready (meaning when you're in the copy room ready to retrieve your documents). Welcome back to warm and fuzzy.

# Save It for Your Eyes Only

In Word, Excel, or any other Office application, a section in the Print dialog box lets you tell the printer to hold off printing your document until you're in the copy room. However, where to set this up depends on the type of printer you're using. The shared printer I make use of is a specific type of Xerox brand, and I can show you how to set up secure printing for that one. If you use a different brand of printer (such as Hewlett-Packard, Epson, or whatever), poke around in the Print dialog box and see how you can make sure the document you're sending off can be securely printed. Reading the manual or going to the printer company's Web site can also prove fruitful.

To print securely on a Xerox printer:

1. On the **File** menu, click **Print**.

2. On the **Print** dialog box, click **Properties**, and then click **Advanced**.

3. Under **Job type**, select **Secure Print**. You will be asked to type a four-digit code twice.

4. Go to your printer, select your print job, and then type the same four-digit code.

**Note**   The procedure described here is a general one; the actual procedure might differ for your specific model of Xerox printer.

The printers that offer secure printing options have slightly different ways of accessing that feature. So again, I suggest that you read the documentation to get an idea of how (not to mention if) your particular printer can manage this sort of task.

So please, save yourself, your documents, and your irregular running gait any embarrassing moments. It takes just a few minutes to figure out how to print securely, and then you can spend your exercise time at the gym or, better yet, go outside and get some fresh air.

Chapter Six

# Making the Most of Performance Reviews

*Nobody can make you feel inferior without your consent.*

— *Eleanor Roosevelt*

Chances are that if you work for a living, you're going to experience the joy of being reviewed on the work you do. That's right: performance reviews, that time of year again, the dreaded season when every conversation with your coworkers and your manager is laden with innuendo and suspicion, causing your paranoid tendencies to bubble to the surface...

# Everyone Takes Part in Performance Reviews

Performance reviews (or whatever your company calls them), are just part—if an unpleasant part—of being an employee. You can take steps to make sure you're ready for them.

Whether you're the fly-under-the-radar type of employee, the showoff star performer, or the manager who has to deliver bad news, reviews can be scary and downright nerve-racking. However, there are ways to make performance reviews—for the giver and the receiver—a little less overwhelming.

Let's see if Microsoft Office and I can't share some of your burden and ease your troubled mind. Of course, if you have nothing to worry about, why are you so troubled?

# Using Search Folders to Keep Track of Your Great Work

A great way to see what you've done all year long is to go through status reports and e-mail communications with your clients, your managers, and your coworkers and then pick out the most glowing accomplishments. Sure, you can go through your Sent Items folder and read through each e-mail message, but that could take days, and you're likely to miss something really good. Maybe you even had the foresight to pop these e-mail messages into a special folder, but it's possible that you've forgotten which message is in what folder. There is an easier way: Microsoft Office Outlook Search Folders.

---

**Note**   Search Folders are available in Office Outlook 2003 and later versions.

---

Search Folders are virtual views of messages that are stored elsewhere. Use them to keep track of important information you need on hand.

Search Folders (as you saw in Chapter 4, "Surviving Life in the Office") are virtual folders that contain e-mail messages that match specific criteria you've previously set up. By *virtual*, I mean that these folders aren't where messages are actually stored; instead, these folders contain just *links* to these e-mail messages so that you can access specific messages for a particular reason. Let me explain with an example. (I didn't understand the concept until someone did this for me, too.)

## How Crabby Uses Search Folders to Get Raises and Bonuses

I'm not sure how your manager keeps up with all that you do, but I'm required to send a weekly status report—in e-mail—to my manager. It lists the tasks I've accomplished during the week, what my plans are for next week, how many people have come by my office to complain about me or my column, and how many readers wrote to ask me whether the Crabby Office Assistant was available for download (as if Crabby were akin to an animated paper clip or kitty cat—oh, please!!!).

I've created a Search Folder named Status Reports. I set up this folder so that whenever I send an e-mail message containing the term *Status*, a virtual view of this message automatically appears in this Search Folder, while the real copy of the message stays in my Sent Items folder. I've set up my Status Reports Search Folder so that if the phrase *Status Reports* appears in the subject field alone *or* just in the body of an e-mail message (if I forgot to add something to the subject line, which, of course, I wouldn't do), this message will appear in the Status Reports Search Folder. You, however, can choose whatever criteria you want, including messages that have been flagged for importance and messages sent to a certain person. That way, I don't ever have to go looking for status reports if I want to refer to them. Links to all the reports are in this folder, and I can pluck out my accomplishments and drop them onto my performance review (and, of course, leave out the not-so-great stuff like "Dear Crabby, you've lost your edge and I think you're not being crabby enough.")

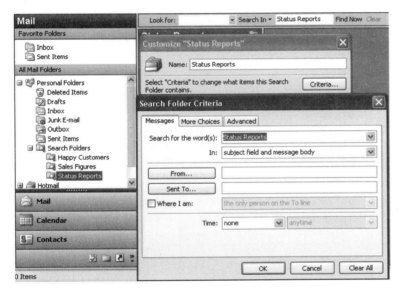

Of course, you can set up as many Search Folders as you want (up to 20) for as many reasons as you can think of, depending on the type of work you do. For example, if you're a project manager, you can have a Search Folder related to specific project developments. If you're a salesperson, you can set up a few Search Folders that mirror the e-mail messages containing sales results and figures. And if you're a customer service representative, you can set up a Search Folder that tracks customer satisfaction e-mail messages.

Now, suppose you don't really get e-mail messages regarding the work you do. In that case, you could create an e-mail message—perhaps with something in the Subject line that matches the criteria of a Search Folder you've set up—and then send it to yourself.

Whatever your work is and however your performance reviews are set up, you can use Search Folders in Outlook to make sure that the work you do doesn't go unnoticed.

Take the free Microsoft Office Training course, "Search Folders: The Easy Way to Find, Read, and Organize Your E-Mail," available at go.microsoft.com/fwlink/?LinkId=60968

# Being a Goody-Goody: Show Off Your Skills

One great way to show your manager just how irreplaceable you are is by becoming more knowledgeable about the work you do. You can do this in a variety of ways, depending on what sort of company you work for and what type of work you do.

I can tell you that Microsoft (just like many other high-striving companies, I imagine), values employee growth. This could mean taking online training courses (either internal or external), going to seminars, reading books specific to our job, or getting better at using the tools we use every day to get our work done—namely, Microsoft Office.

## Become a Microsoft Office Specialist

Something to consider, when proving that you've grown as an employee throughout the year, is getting the Microsoft Office Specialist (MOS) certification, a globally recognized standard for demonstrating desktop computer skills. In other words, whether you're an existing employee or someone looking for a job, having this certification can give you an edge: it tells employers, hiring managers, and in this case, your current manager that you're good at making the most of Office programs. And let's face it, most workplaces do use Word, Excel, PowerPoint, and many of the other Office programs.

And if you have taken the time to get certified, chances are that'll look good on your performance review (not to mention make you a more efficient Office user).

You've taken the time to really study and get to know a program that you use on an everyday basis. A MOS certificate proves that you're worth your weight in gold (not to mention salary).

Basically, the certification course is like grade school, middle school, high school, trade school, or college all over again: you study the material, you regurgitate what you've learned, and when you pass the test, you get a good grade, a gold star, a diploma (and, perhaps, a higher-paying job).

In plain terms, you study for the test, you pass the test, and you're considered an expert in that program—it's that simple. Each Office program has its own exam, so you don't have to be super-knowledgeable in each and every program. You can take just the exams for the programs that you work with the most, or the ones you want to become certified in, or even the ones you want to learn. When you pass, you get a nice, professional-looking certificate, and you've earned the right to have your own cable news show (or at least strut around the office spouting your opinions about mail merge, revision marks, document sharing, and data analysis).

But beyond the bragging rights and the smug smile of satisfaction you're wearing, earning MOS certification comes with these more useful perks:

**You'll increase your productivity.** Even if you're already gainfully employed, being certified is bound to make you more confident, efficient, and competent at your job. (Hint: Managers like those kinds of things.)

**You'll improve relations with your employees.** If you're the manager, encouraging your coworkers to become certified will let them know that you want them to keep learning and keep getting better at their jobs. Sure, they'll see through your intentions (Work faster! Work harder! Work smarter!), but they'll understand that everyone wins in this situation (Faster, harder, smarter equals better. Better equals recognition. Recognition equals prestige, money, fame, and so on).

Now, regarding your performance review, including scanned images of these certificates in your review document might be overkill, but hey, who's going to turn you down for that promotion now? Go on, get certified, and prove your Office prowess.

Interested in becoming a Microsoft Office Specialist? Visit the Microsoft Office Specialist Web site at go.microsoft.com/fwlink/?LinkId=60971.

# Take a Training Course on Office Online

There are scads and scads (I can't tell you the exact number, because more are being created each day) of free online training courses available to you on the Office Online Web site. And, just like studying for your MOS exam, taking a training course can only serve to make you a better Office user and therefore a more efficient and productive worker. And while that means big bucks to your manager and employer, what it can mean for you is less time at your desk and more time with your family, on the slopes, sitting in a wicker chair and sipping a margarita, or however you like to spend your time away from work.

## Navigating the Office Training Home Page

Just like the Office Templates home page, the Training home page offers a few ways to find the training course you need. You can browse training courses by Office program, and you can also peek at some of the "staff picks"—courses that the experts think are extra-valuable to you.

And just like the Template home page, the training team presents three rotating course picks under the headings "Built by Request," "What's Hot," and "Featured Course." These are courses that Office customers have suggested, that have been deemed quite useful (based on the number of people who've taken the course), or that the training team has just created or finds relevant to what's going on this season.

You can also click links that take you to demos, Webcasts, and skill assessment resources, and for each course, you can see how the course has been rated by others who've taken it.

Like I mentioned, there are many free training courses available to you. Some are designed for you beginners, still learning your way around the Office products, while others are for you more experienced and seasoned Office users.

---

**Tip**   Whether you're new to Office or new to Office Training (or both), I suggest that you read "Beginner's Training for Office 2003" (go.microsoft.com/fwlink /?LinkId=60964) before you jump right in there and start training to your hearts' desire. This article tells you a bit about why you might need some training, what some of the available courses are, and how to get started.

---

## Sample Office Training Courses for Beginners

You might be new to Microsoft Office or just new to the many Office training courses that Microsoft offers. Whichever your situation, taking a few beginner courses is a great way to jump in and start becoming a better Office user as well as a way to familiarize yourself with all that the training courses can offer you.

Here are a few sample courses for people new to Microsoft PowerPoint, Microsoft Excel, and Microsoft FrontPage. After you take these courses, you'll be ready for something a bit more advanced.

### Create Your First Presentation (PowerPoint)
(go.microsoft.com/fwlink/?LinkId=40405)

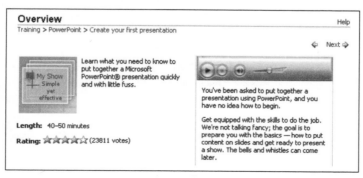

### Audio Course: Get to Know Excel: Create Your First Workbook

(go.microsoft.com/fwlink/?LinkId=60956)

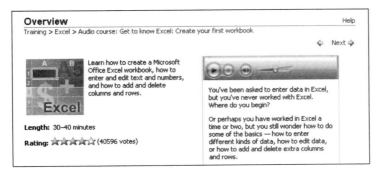

### Hyperlinks I: The Basics (FrontPage)    (go.microsoft.com/fwlink/?LinkId=60962)

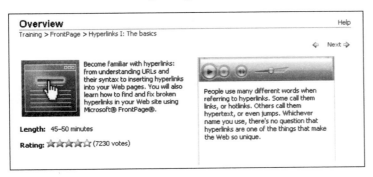

## Sample Office Training Courses for You Big Shots

Once you've taken a few courses and mastered the basics, you're ready to move on:

### Charts III: Customize a Professional-Looking Chart (Excel)

(go.microsoft.com/fwlink/?LinkId=60965)

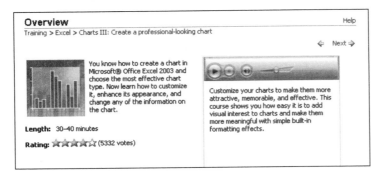

**Audio Course: Revise Documents with Track Changes and Comments (Word)**
(go.microsoft.com/fwlink/?LinkId=60966)

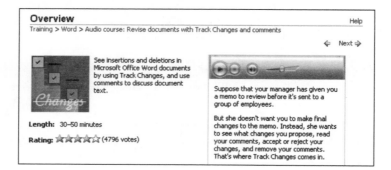

**Animations III: Timing (PowerPoint)**   (go.microsoft.com/fwlink/?LinkId=60967)

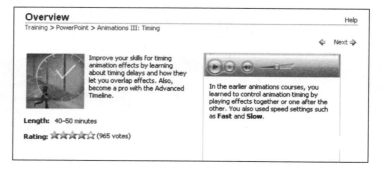

Pique your interest? Take a gander at all the online, self-paced training courses on Office Online, at go.microsoft.com/fwlink/?LinkId=25327.

# When You're the Manager

While I'm not a manager myself (nor am I particularly manageable), I do understand that it's a burden to be almighty and powerful. So let me imagine that I am someone who does have some power over who gets the raise and who gets the boot.

## Let a Template Do the Hard Part

Whether you're going to deliver good or bad news during an employee performance review, there's an Office template to help you. And if you want your underlings to show you their progress over the past year, there's a template for that, too. In fact, Office provides templates for just about any situation for any type of business. Here are just a few examples:

**Computer/People-Management Skills Assessment**   (go.microsoft.com/fwlink /?LinkId=60973) This template is a predefined form that not only helps employees capture, in one fell swoop, their current skill-set, but also provides space for them to start a skill development plan.

**Interpersonal/Organizational Skills Assessment**   (go.microsoft.com/fwlink /?LinkId=56909) If you require your employees to perform a self-assessment of their job performance to help evaluate where they're doing well ("Always on time!") and where they need improvement ("Constantly berating tardy employees!"), this is a great template to use to gather and record employee capabilities within different categories.

**Performance Interview Planning Checklist**   (go.microsoft.com/fwlink/?LinkId=56910) This one is for you, the manager. It offers a list of questions for you to ask your employees during that big review meeting. And just as you can with any other Office templates, you can customize this checklist by adding or deleting questions that pertain to a specific employee and the kind of work he or she does.

---

**Tip**   To download a performance evaluation and status report template and customize it to suit your needs, go to go.microsoft.com/fwlink/?LinkId=60970.

---

# The Right to Privacy: Use Information Rights Management

When you're a manager or Human Resources professional, keeping information confidential is critical (to you, to the employees you're working with, and to your reputation). If e-mail is your main way of sharing confidential information (such as performance reviews), consider using Information Rights Management (IRM). IRM was introduced in Office 2003, and its main purpose is to give you more control over who can open, copy, edit, print, and even forward these types of messages.

---

**Note**   You can use IRM to create content with restricted permissions in Office 2003, Word 2003, Excel 2003, and PowerPoint 2003.

---

Consider this scenario: You have received an employee's performance review via a Word document attached to an e-mail message. Chances are, this person has taken a lot of time and effort to write about the big accounts he's landed, the hours he's put in, the marriage that fell apart because of all of this work, and so on. In other words, there is a lot of confidential information in this thing. And then you, being the dutiful manager you are, have put in quite a bit of time yourself acknowledging his work, responding to his remarks, turning him down for a promotion...

Well, you know how you sometimes mistype someone's e-mail address or internal e-mail alias? What happens if you sent your review to the wrong person? (I'll tell you what: a lot of back-pedaling, embarrassment, and frantic "recall message" prayers, that's what.)

If you're using IRM, the person who received this message, the one who wasn't supposed to, won't be able to open it because that person wasn't given the right to— by you. That's one of the beauties of IRM: the e-mail message is available only to the people you assigned it to.

---

To learn more about how to restrict access to documents, go to go.microsoft.com/fwlink/?LinkId=60972.

---

When you send an e-mail message using IRM, your recipients will not be able to open it until their credentials have been checked (nor will they be able to read the message's contents in the reading pane). When they double-click the e-mail message to open it, a little box pops up while their credentials are being checked. It's just a way to let the recipients know what's going on.

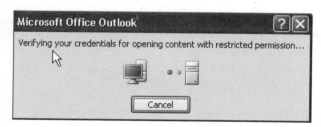

---

**Note** Even if your recipients don't have Office 2003, they can download a free program that will allow them to view a message sent using IRM—they'll be prompted to download the program when they try to view the e-mail message.

# Final Words of Advice

A performance review—no matter what your company calls it—can be a great tool for measuring and identifying your or your employees' successes, strengths, and areas for growth. But keep in mind that trying to document what you (or your worker bees) did all year (or over the past six months, or however frequently this event rolls around) in one frantic day of gathering information is probably not the best approach. Pace yourself. Try some of the tips provided in this chapter, and then think up some techniques of your own.

I do hope that you get that promotion/raise/window office you were counting on. If it doesn't happen this time around, remember that Crabby is still proud of you. Now get back to work, show some pluck, and prove your worth.

Chapter Seven

# Working It from Home: Tips for Telecommuters

*If you are idle, be not solitary; if you are solitary, be not idle.*

*— Samuel Johnson*

Working from home might seem like a fuzzy-slippered fantasy come true, and many of you who have never actually participated in this kind of setup have an image in your head that involves you, those slippers, a homemade latte, and a purring cat draped over the monitor. And yes, while you can incorporate those things into your daily workload, having a balanced approach is the only way to make this telecommuting thing really work.

# Telecommuting: Myth vs. Fact

Telecommuting (or working from home, or as some people like to call it, "working it from home") has become quite the trend as remote technology gets better, fuel prices and traffic gridlock stress levels continue to rise, and companies start to realize that workers can be productive without Big Brother watching their every move.

I've already mentioned the casual attire, ready access to the refrigerator, and your favorite creature at your side.

Well, my friends...SNAP OUT OF IT! It's time to awaken from that dream and dismiss those fantasies about telecommuting. Are you ready? We're going to debunk the myths and get right to the facts.

## Myth #1. You'll have lots of free time on your hands.

## Fact

Now that you don't have coworkers or a boss breathing the same air as you, it can be challenging to stay focused. Limiting distractions (yes, Bill Maher reruns and the Oprah show count as distractions) can be one of the toughest tasks you've ever had to complete on your daily to-do list. It takes time to learn how to manage your time on your own, so prepare for that period of adjustment.

See, if you don't buckle down, focus, and take this seriously from the get-go, you may find your work-related procrastination manifesting itself in superorganized closets, a spotless (and again, superorganized) refrigerator, or a worn-out dog dreading one more walk around the block. (I can tell you—from experience—that at times even cleaning up after the Crabby Office Dog more than once a day can start to sound pretty good compared to writing a status report.)

If any of these things start to happen, you may find yourself with more free time than you ever expected, since you'll be out of a job. (Hence, the myth of free time is not necessarily a myth, now is it?)

## Myth #2. You need to become an über-gadget-geek and set up your home office to handle every techno-trick that comes your way.

## Fact

Unless you plan to be a telecommuting crime fighter, setting up your home office with what you'd normally have at your work office is probably sufficient (and of course, what you need depends on the type of job you do). A desk, a chair, high-speed Internet access, a working computer with good security (your company should require this anyway), software that is compatible with what the rest of the company is using, and a door that closes (and preferably locks) is usually a good place to start. A phone dedicated to only work-related calls might be a good idea, too. Again, I speak from experience (and I have the cell phone bills to prove it).

Once you're in the swing of things, you'll figure out what you need and don't need, and your company should be able to help out with that. Remember: you don't want to spend on gadgets what you're saving in transportation costs.

## Myth #3. Everyone wants to work from home.

## Fact

This simply isn't true. Not everyone is clamoring to telecommute. A lot of people like the idea of coming into the office, seeing their coworkers, and taking part in the gossip, the office politics, and the Friday afternoon Bacchanalian revelry (that everyone, on Monday morning, pretends never happened). Maybe you're one of these people. Maybe you're just more comfortable with the customary coming into the office on a daily basis, taking your breaks at breaktime, taking your lunch at lunchtime, fraternizing with the people you work with, and punching out at the end of the day. There's nothing wrong with that—in fact, most employers count on your being there. So don't give in to the craze of telecommuting if it doesn't feel right for you—it isn't for everyone.

## Myth #4. No more childcare costs!

## Fact

While this myth might seem obviously untrue, I do feel the need to spell it out for you. You might pride yourself on being the ultimate multitasker, with the ability to juggle sales reports, group meetings, and diaper changes (with games of Candyland thrown in there somewhere)—all within the same 9-to-5 schedule. But while your children may be covered by your health benefits (not to mention a joy to be around—most of the time), they are not part of this deal (and I think you know that). Just as if you were working away from the home, you need to figure out what to do with the kids. I'm guessing that most employers will want to know your child-care (or elder-care) arrangements before you set up this telecommuting agreement. And believing that you can just take care of the children during the day and do your work at night is also not the way to go. Your work will suffer, and your daytime absence will be noticed (as will those dark circles under your eyes).

As everyone (or at least everyone who has a child) knows, raising and caring for children is a full-time job in itself. That whole "it takes a village" thing is a nice sentiment, but as you and I both know, sometimes the village is you, Bert & Ernie, and the disembodied voice of your mother or best friend on the phone. And so, at the risk of raising the hackles of every employed and not-employed parent everywhere (and I suppose that covers all the bases of all the parents out there), you cannot be a full-time telecommuter and a stay-at-home parent. If you've figured out a part-time deal with your company, great. But if you're expected to be doing company-related work on company time, I suggest you fulfill that obligation.

This leads to the final myth...

## Myth #5. You're the Lone Ranger, doing your own job with your own horse on your own time.

### Fact

Unless you're the boss, you aren't the Lone Ranger; you're Tonto (and anyway, even the "boss" plays Tonto to someone). Make sure that you regularly check in with the person who actually *is* your Lone Ranger. And while you're at it, stay in touch with your coworkers, too. They may forget you exist. This could mean visiting the office for important meetings or making good use of some of the Office technologies such as Live Meeting, Document Workspaces, or OneNote shared note-taking sessions.

### Office Technologies for Telecommuters

While Live Meeting, SharePoint, and OneNote shared note-taking sessions are great tools for collaborating with people from afar, they are not designed to be eternal substitutes for the real thing: face-to-face contact. If your job requires that you see your coworkers, your manager, or your customers on a daily basis, reconsider your telecommuting dreams. Or if you still want to telecommute, think about doing it on a part-time basis.

## Using Microsoft Office Collaboration Tools to Stay Connected

Even if you're not in the room—in person, that is—for meetings and collaboration sessions, that doesn't mean you can't "be" there...virtually. Microsoft Office offers a variety of collaboration solutions that enable you and your meeting leaders to work together. I've called out the three that I find the most compelling and easy to use: Live

Meeting, Document Workspaces, and OneNote shared note-taking sessions.

# Live Meeting

Live Meeting is a great tool, not just for telecommuters, but also for people on the go in general. In a nutshell, Live Meeting is a way to hold or take part in meetings in real time. All you need is a live person, a phone, and an Internet connection (and yes, of course, something interesting to share).

Here's how it works: When you host a meeting in Live Meeting, you invite whomever you want (up to 2,000 people) by using Microsoft Office Outlook. Your invitees receive your Outlook meeting invitations, which contain a unique meeting URL and a password. When the meeting is set to begin, they head on over to the URL and sign in.

**Join Meeting**

To join a meeting, type a Display Name as you want it to appear to others in the meeting. Enter a Meeting ID and Meeting Key (if required by the meeting organizer), and then click Join Meeting.

| | |
|---|---|
| Name: | Crabby |
| Meeting ID: | ReaderTips |
| Meeting Key (if required): | •••••• |

**Join Meeting**

By using the Microsoft Office Live Meeting service you agree that at any time during this meeting any presenter may initiate the recording function, which will result in your conversation and communications being recorded and logged by Office Live Meeting. If you do not agree to recording, please exit Microsoft Office Live Meeting.

Live Meeting meetings are interactive; they allow anyone to review, discuss, or add notes to any printable file. What this means, for example, is that if you're using a PowerPoint presentation, you just bring up that presentation on your screen, and everyone who is dialed in can see what you're seeing. If you're all on the phone together during a Live Meeting, people can interrupt and ask questions, and you can address those questions before moving on to the next slide. If you're hosting with Live Meeting, you can also set it up so that everyone can collaborate—by using the drawing tools to call out important points on those PowerPoint slides, for example. It's simple, it's easy to set up, and it's a really great way to collaborate from afar. You can host (or be a part of) training seminars or team meetings, give an interactive sales demo, or even hold a virtual press conference. In other words, whatever you want to show, you can show it using this technology. It's one of the best ways I know to both show what you're up to and be a part of what everyone else is doing, too.

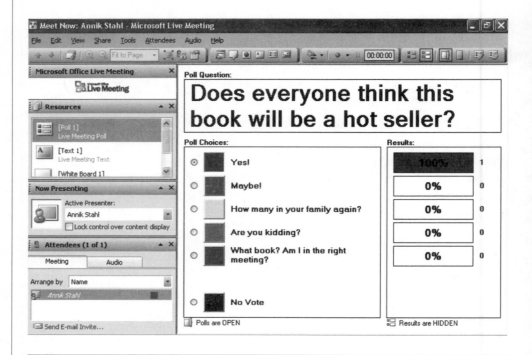

For more information about Live Meeting, visit go.microsoft.com/fwlink /?LinkId=35524.

## Document Workspaces

A Document Workspace is a Microsoft Windows SharePoint Services site that allows everyone with permissions to work on a document, add their own documents, and even receive notifications when the documents they're interested in have been changed.

One of the most common ways to create a Document Workspace is to use e-mail to send a document as a shared attachment. When you add a file to an e-mail message, you have the option to send the file as a regular attachment, which means that everyone gets a separate copy of the attachment. If you choose to send a shared attachment, using the Shared Workspace task pane, you type a URL of where the document will be stored on the SharePoint site.

**Note**   When you use the Shared Workspace task pane, you can create Document Workspaces in Microsoft Office Word 2003, Microsoft Office Excel 2003, Microsoft Office PowerPoint 2003, and Microsoft Office Visio 2003 (and later versions) only.

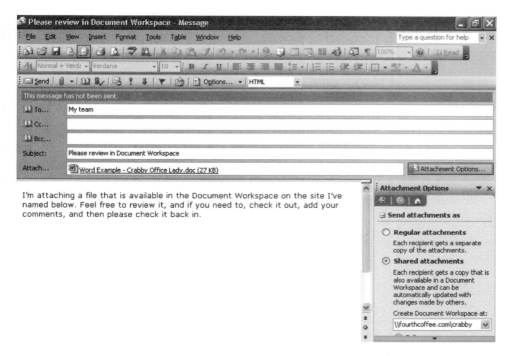

You can also bypass the e-mail part and use commands on your SharePoint site to create a Document Workspace. Just let your participants know that you've given them access to this part of the site and be sure to set up whatever permissions they have (reader, writer, editor, lurker ...).

For more information about how to create a Document Workspace, visit go.microsoft.com/fwlink/?LinkId=61475.

## OneNote Shared Note-Taking Sessions

As you may or may not know (from reading my columns about OneNote), I'm a *huge* fan of this program. Frankly, it's my favorite Office program, and if I could write only about OneNote, I probably would. I use it for just about everything—to jot down column ideas, to keep track of customer feedback (the good, the bad, the ugly), to make personal notes having to do with my daughter's school functions and birthday gift ideas, and yes, even to make notes about ideas for this book.

But as a sometime telecommuter, I find one feature in OneNote particularly invaluable: the shared note-taking session. When I have an issue with something my column editor has sent me (me? editing problems?) or perhaps need to brainstorm with my manager about his notes in my performance review (grrr...), instead of sending a formal e-mail, I can invite these two guys (and yes, they are both guys) to a OneNote shared note-taking session.

Here's how it works: When your computer is connected to the Internet or a network, you and the participants you have invited (or who have invited you) can view and work on each other's notes together. It's a virtual whiteboard, if you will (and once you try it out, you *will*). You can add notes in handwriting, by typing them in, and you can even use the drawing tools to circle important points.

You can share a single page of notes, a section, or even your entire notebook. (Be careful here—if you're like me, there are some personal items contained in your OneNote notebook.) You just select the pages you want to share and then invite the participants.

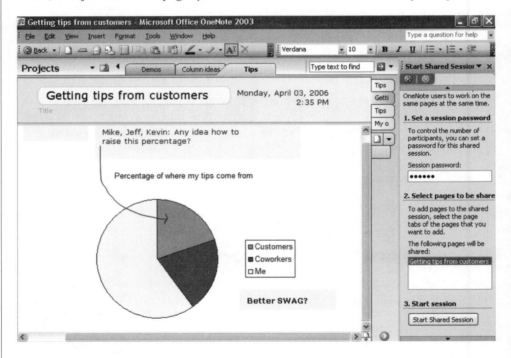

If you're using Outlook (and I know you are), you can invite people by using an e-mail message that is automatically created. This Outlook message contains the invitation to the session, the IP address of your computer (so that your invitees can connect), and even a password, which you can set up if you want to include it in that message.

---

For more information about OneNote shared note-taking sessions, read go.microsoft.com/fwlink/?LinkId=61477. If you want to see how this feature works, feast your eyes on this demo: go.microsoft.com/fwlink/?LinkId=61476.

---

OK, so maybe your company isn't quite so on board as to have these collaboration tools at its disposal. Or maybe you don't want to look up those Web addresses and actually learn something new about collaborating from afar. (Hey, relax. I'm not here to judge— I'm just here to suggest.)

That doesn't mean you're off the hook, though, fella. Call in often, send status reports to your manager, and if you're so inclined, ask him or her to forward the juicy and related parts on to your team. That way, your coworkers will get an idea of what you're doing and how fantastically you're doing it, and you might even raise the productivity bar for all of them in the process.

# Is Telecommuting Right for You? A Checklist

Now that we've separated myth from fact and I've given you plenty of opportunity to research the various collaboration tools at your disposal, you know that working from home isn't for everyone. If you're prone to distraction or procrastination, or if you live for the daily drama around the water cooler, perhaps you ought to reconsider jumping into this type of agreement between you and your employer. But if you think you may be right for this type of work, ask yourself the following questions:

- Are you self-motivated and organized? Can you set up a self-imposed daily structure and stick to it? Do you even want to?

- Can you limit the distractions around you (personal phone calls, bickering kids, the fish swimming around in its bowl, goading you to contemplate a simpler life)?

- Do you have the necessary workspace and tools to make your particular job workable from afar? This could mean an office separate from the rest of your house, a laptop or desktop that you can take away from the workplace, a reliable Internet connection, and all the tools you need to get on to the company intranet.

- Can you work without someone imposing structure on you? Can you create your own structure just as easily—and stick to it? Again, do you even want to?

- Do you have someone to take care of the kids while you take care of the business? (See myth #4.)

- Do you have a room where you can close the door to distractions?

- Do you have friends and family who can understand that just because you're home doesn't mean you're in "home mode"?

If you've answered a resounding "Yes!" to most of these questions, chances are you'd make a decent telecommuter.

## A Few Tips for Telecommuters

Now that we've debunked some of the more common myths about working from a home office (and you still want to pursue this situation), here are a few tips to keep you going:

**Get out of the house once in a while.**   We humans are a social species, which means that having some form of contact with each other is necessary for our health and sanity. While you may feel terribly "lone wolf" sometimes, getting out of the house is still a good idea, if only to breathe some fresh air. And for a change of pace, you can take your work with you to a local café that has a chair and table, an outlet for your laptop, and even better, wireless Internet access (and great scones).

**Mind your manners while you're out of the house.**   Regarding that previous tip: if you're going to sit in the same spot all day at that local café, make sure that you actually purchase something—coffee, one or two of those great scones, a soy smoothie, whatever. The owners of these places don't make a living by admiring the sound of your fingers clickety-clacking across the keyboard day in and day out. You're making the big bucks sitting there (or at the very least, having a bit of freedom), so don't be afraid to spend a bit of it and share the love (and the coffee breath).

**Stay in touch with work.**   No man is an island, no woman is an isthmus (or something like that). You rely on your manager and your coworkers just as they rely on you. So stay in touch. Make sure that you have a phone line that is just for work (and perhaps a fax line or access to an online fax service, too), be available during normal business hours, and get your work done on time. Also, be sure to make—and keep—appointments. You'd do this if you were working in the office, so don't slack off once you're a disembodied voice on the phone. Oh, and if you can attend team meetings in person, consider doing so. If you can't, call in, and better yet, encourage the meeting organizer to make use of Live Meeting. Everyone will appreciate your efforts, and you'll be a good example of how telecommuting can work.

**Expect a period of adjustment.**   Of the telecommuters I've surveyed (including myself), I can tell you that every one of us has had to go through a period of adjustment when we felt downright isolated and even lonesome. One coworker even said he felt such acute empathy and anxiety for his son's single fish that he ended up buying it a friend. (The "friend" promptly ate the original fish, but that's another story for another day—and don't you dare tell the son that his beloved fish is really a murdering, smug-faced imposter.)

Seriously, though, if you're not comfortable being alone, telecommuting isn't for you. If you're beginning to compare yourself to a fish swimming alone in a bowl, telecommuting isn't for you. If you're taking too many trips to stare at the contents of the fridge, telecommuting isn't for you. But if these are all passing things or one-time incidents, give yourself some time and know that working from home will take some getting used to.

## Is Your Company on Board?

Now that you're ready for telecommuting, is your company? Many companies have their own policies regarding telecommuting. Some companies flat-out forbid it. But, hey, even if that's the case, maybe you can be the pioneering rogue.

Consider this approach: If you're really bent on this telecommuting thing, write up a proposal that outlines the specific points of the whys, the wheres, the hows, and the...whatevers. Maybe your company hasn't considered telecommuting as a good alternative because it hasn't ever had a good reason to—maybe no one has created such a well-thought-out proposal encouraging the company to contemplate and provide for such an arrangement. Creativity, self-motivation, and a new way of looking at things can only serve to make you stand out from the crowd.

Maybe you're that one person who will demonstrate that telecommuting isn't just good for you, it's good for the company and good for the environment. (Even if it turned out not so good for my coworker's son's *original* fish—at least another live creature got to experience life outside the pet shop.)

Chapter Eight

# Crabby's Getting-Away-from-It-All Checklist

*Vacation is what you take when you can't take what you've been taking any longer.*

*— The Cowardly Lion (From L. Frank Baum, The Wizard of Oz)*

Going on vacation or taking a leave of absence from work can be a great way to recharge your batteries, get out of the rat race for a while, and get a fresh outlook on both your life and your work. It's healthy, and it's necessary. Yet I do understand that sometimes your getting away might not come at the best time for you or the people with (or for) whom you work, particularly if it's not for a personal vacation—if an illness or a family emergency is involved.

# Make a Plan for a Stress-Free Return to Work

Whatever your reasons (and however they arise), being away from the office, unless you have a clear plan for how to get back into the swing of things once you return, might be more trouble than it was worth. I mean, can you imagine the e-mail messages, tasks, meeting requests, and unfinished business that will await you? But don't panic—a little preparation can go a long way.

In this chapter, we're going to cover two basic challenges:

As Benjamin Franklin said, *"Employ thy time well, if thou meanest to get leisure."*

- How to take care of your coworkers, your workload, and your e-mail Inbox (and by default, yourself), while you're away
- How to return with grace and less stress than you might imagine

### *Everyone* Needs to Get Away from It All

I am not a manager. I manage no one (save for my daughter, and even then I'm not sure who is managing whom). My point here is that everyone, wherever they reside on the ladder of influence (and I know that you know the "ladder" to which I'm trying to gracefully refer), is probably managed by someone. (Well, perhaps Bill Gates is not "managed" by someone *at* Microsoft, but he does have a wife and kids, and so, well, you can see what I'm implying.)

And so? My point? My point is that everyone—from your basic drones (that'd be me) to your middle managers to your executives—needs to get away. People need time away from work—time to regroup and refresh their brains and their hearts.

Most companies know this; they know that stressed out and exhausted employees do not work to their potential. Consider your next employer's vacation benefits before you jump right into a new job that takes you away—forever—from the things that make you *you*: your hobbies, your passions, your family, your friends, and your vacation time.

Put simply: How can you prepare to go away? How plugged in do you want to be while you're away? How can you prepare before you go so that once you've returned you're not so overwhelmed that you're ready to flee again? (This last question assumes that you don't end up like the artist Paul Gauguin, spending the rest of your life painting the beautiful women of Tahiti.)

## The Reasons We Need to Get Away from the Office

Before we get into my basic ideas about how to prepare to go on leave or go on vacation, I want to mention the different types of leave that we worker bees take (and yes, *worker bees* include managers and managers of managers) and the different things we need to take care of before we go.

## The Vacation Getaway

If it's a vacation we're talking about here, you might be fanatical about every little detail surrounding your holiday plans. For example, you use (and if you're like most Americans, probably overuse) a credit card. And if you're smart, that card earns you airline miles. You check—and recheck—every travel Web site to make sure you're getting the best deals on airfare, hotels, guided tours, and car rentals. You read reviews and watch all the TV shows that offer glimpses of your dream destination. You make sure your pet is taken care of—in the manner to which he, she, or it has become accustomed. You know how early you need to arrive at the airport, who is taking you there, and the status of his or her driving record. In other words, you are prepared, Mr. or Ms. Type A.

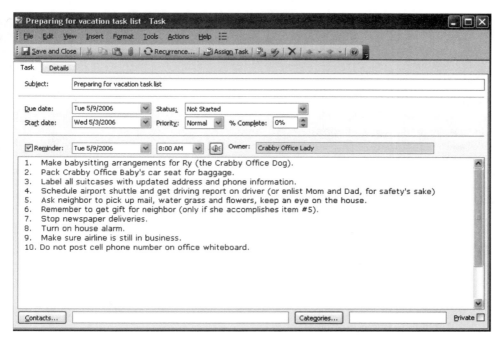

OK, so perhaps I'm exaggerating a bit, but I'm guessing that you recognize yourself—at least somewhat—in the preceding paragraph. Listen, I'm not saying that taking those extra steps to make sure that your vacation goes as planned is a bad thing. In fact, it's necessary. But this chapter is not about how to plan your vacation—no, I'm pretty sure you can handle that on your own. (And I'm not the Crabby Vacation Planner. If I were, your vacation would include overnight stays in airports with one working restroom and roadside motels with stinky carpets and grumpy front desk managers.)

So...a vacation is one type of way to get away from work.

# When You're Taking a Leave of Absence

Most companies have a clear policy about how much vacation you accrue during the year. You probably have that policy memorized and most likely knew the exact number of days that were yours to be free even before you signed on as a new employee.

However, if you have decided to take a leave of absence (or if a situation or scenario has precipitated this necessity for you), you might not be clear about your company's policies regarding this issue. Before you find yourself in this position (and never—never *ever*—say never, my friends), take some time to find out what the guidelines are for your organization.

## When You're a Working Parent

Things have changed in the workplace. Some women decide to leave their careers—temporarily or otherwise—to care for their kids during the day. Some men do this, too. But many parents can't afford—or don't want to—leave their careers. Whatever your situation, if you have a family, it takes a great deal of energy, planning, and, frankly, *money* to make sure that your children are in the care of someone you trust.

If you've decided to take some time off work to start (or continue) your family—whether it be through pregnancy, adoption, or through foster care—taking the steps to ensure that your job is still going to be there when your off-time is over takes a bit of planning. But it's not impossible to prepare for this, especially if your company values you as a worker as well as a functioning and caring member of society.

On that note, look into the Family Medical Leave Act (www.dol.gov/esa/whd/fmla). FMLA is a U.S. federal law that requires employers to allow eligible employees a specific amount of leave time for certain family (as well as medical) reasons during a 12-month period. Every company has its own FMLA-compliance policies; be sure that you understand where your employer stands with regard to this law.

**Find out what your company's policies are regarding an extended leave.** What is your company's return-to-work policy? How will this impact your benefits and pay? Do you need to set an unalterable start and end date? Does your company even provide short-term leave options? These are great things to know about before you even consider taking a leave of absence. And because your specific circumstance might be an emergency, these are good things to know about a company even before you start working for it.

So before you start planning your exit strategy, make sure you know all the rules and regulations and perhaps schedule some time with your Human Resources representative. These folks are experts at this sort of thing and should have some great ideas about how to prepare for your leave. I can tell you that Microsoft assigns an HR representative to every employee, and it's easy enough to find out who that person is. I, for one, appreciate this resource, and it makes me feel that the company I work for cares about me and what's going on in my life, both inside and outside the office.

**Set up child care** *now.*   If you're about to go on maternity or paternity leave, chances are you're not going to want to be starting the child care research while you're at home recovering from giving birth, dealing with jet lag from an overseas adoption, totally sleep deprived, or all of the above. So try to get ahead and start on that now, before you leave.

Once you are on leave and preparing to come back, even if you've got child care all lined up—whether it be in a daycare/preschool, with a nanny, or with a family member—now's the time to give it several trial runs. It's better to know if something truly won't work now, while you're still on leave, than to have to deal with it when you're back to work. (If it's any consolation, I learned this the hard way.)

Now that we've covered the most common reasons employees need to get away from the office, let's jump into how to prepare for your leave so that when you return, you won't have to deal with the "angry masses" (of e-mail messages in your Inbox and people milling about in your office).

# Before You Go: The Checklist

Your bags are packed, you're ready to go...

Or so you think.

If you're going on vacation, did you alert your newspaper carrier and local post office? Did you turn off the oven? And whether we're talking about a vacation or a leave of absence, did you set your OOF (the "out of the office" message)? Did you deal with tasks, with looming project deadlines, and with meetings (either that you are required to attend or that you yourself have called)? Do your coworkers know that you will be gone? Do your customers know that they will be taken care of by someone else? And is that "someone else" aware of the responsibilities involved?

If you said "yes" to the first two questions, but you're scratching your head about the other items, this chapter is for you. When you're preparing to go on vacation or to take a leave of absence, it's best to take care of some things at the office before you leave.

## Checklist Item #1: Set Up Microsoft Office Outlook to Tell Everyone You Are G-O-N-E

When you're preparing to be away from the office, maybe you're the type who mercilessly pesters everyone with your arrangements (particularly your vacation plans) weeks before you actually leave. (Yes, that is Crabby; I just get so excited that I have to share my enthusiasm with anyone who will listen—whether or not that person is actually listening.) Then you just assume that everyone remembers that you'll be gone for two weeks (or more) and won't send you e-mail.

Wrong. Shocking as it may seem, you are not the center of your coworkers' universe, and it's entirely possible that they will forget that you're gone and send you mail. (Heck, I know a couple of folks who will do it on purpose.) They may even expect you to respond. Wouldn't it be great if your e-mail program—say, Outlook—could send an automatic response that you so craftily created before you left town? One that lets the senders know that you're gone and won't respond to their messages until you're back? There are a couple of ways to do this.

## Using Outlook with Exchange Server

When your company is running Outlook with Exchange Server, you can use a handy feature named the Out Of Office Assistant. This feature lets you create a reply message to e-mail messages sent to you while you're away. From within that feature, you can also set up specific rules about how to file the messages, whom to respond to, how often to reply, and so on.

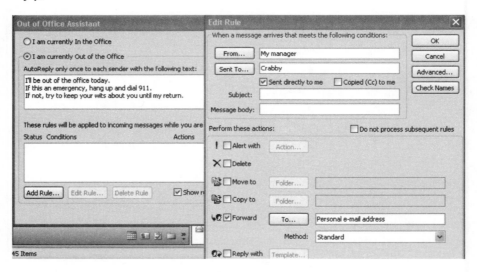

For specific information about how to automatically reply to incoming messages by using Exchange Server (including how to create rules to manage certain conditions), read the article "Automatically Reply to Incoming Messages While Out of the Office" (go.microsoft.com/fwlink/?LinkId=62369).

## Using Outlook Without Exchange Server

That handy Out Of Office Assistant won't appear on the Tools menu if you're not using Outlook with Exchange. (Read that sentence again, please: no Exchange, no Assistant.) However, you're not left out in the cold. If your company is not using Exchange Server, you can combine an Outlook e-mail template with Outlook rules to simulate the functionality of the Out Of Office Assistant.

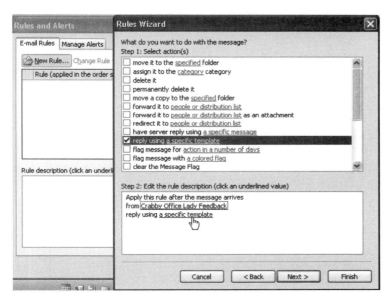

For specific information about how to set up your e-mail account to reply to incoming messages automatically when you're using a POP3 or an IMAP account, read the article "Automatically Reply to Incoming Messages with a POP3 or IMAP E-Mail Account" (go.microsoft.com/fwlink/?LinkId=62367), which will walk you through the procedure, step by step.

Whether you use the Out Of Office Assistant or use a template with a rule, when you create your message (affectionately known as your OOF—for *out of office*), consider mentioning that you're out of the office, note when you'll be returning, and offer the sender another person to contact (if there is anyone) in your absence. If you want to give an alternative number or e-mail address that could be used to track you down, that's up to you. But realize, then, that you're fair game for work-related calls just when you're having the best golf game of your life.

> **To see** how to create an automatic response (using Microsoft Exchange or any other type of e-mail account), watch the demo "Automatically Reply to Messages While Out of the Office," (go.microsoft.com/fwlink/?LinkId=62365). The demo will also show you how to check what type of server—Exchange, POP3, IMAP, and so on—your account uses.

## Checklist Item #2: Block Off Your Office Outlook Calendar

If you use Outlook with Exchange Server, you'll want to mark your Outlook calendar to reflect that you are out of the office.

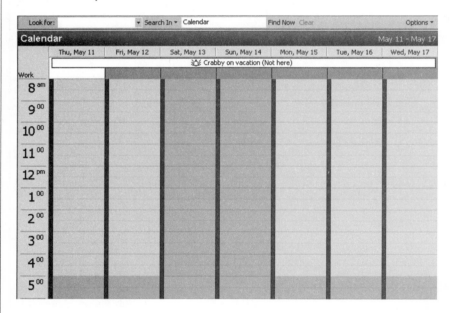

Or if your company doesn't use Exchange Server, consider sending out a broad e-mail message to the people with whom you work the most closely to let them know the dates you'll be out of the office. (Then they can add that information to their calendar by themselves.) That way, if people try to schedule you for yet another meeting, they'll see that you're gone and not available to sit and listen to them yammer on about upcoming reviews, this year's fiscal results, or the boss's pet project that just won't die (at least in his mind). Be sure to remind them to add the dates that you aren't available to their calendar—and set it as *free* time. (That way they'll realize that yes, *they* are free at that time; however, *you* are not.)

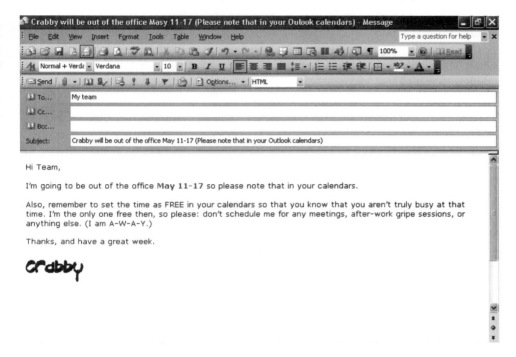

# Checklist Item #3: Decline Standing Meetings

If you're an invitee to meetings that will happen while you're out, the courteous thing to do is decline the meetings. It's also nice to let the organizer know why you won't be attending so that it doesn't seem that your response is a gratuitous "No! I'm not coming! Get over it!"

If you're the organizer of a meeting (recurring or otherwise), send out a cancellation so that 25 people don't show up in a conference room and sit there, vacuously anticipating something happening and someone saying something.

# Checklist Item #4: Check In Files

When you work in a team environment, chances are you participate in a lot of the checking in and checking out of files, which is sort of like how the public library system works: you check a book out of the library and then you check it back in when you have finished with it (so that others can have a go at it). Maybe you do so from a Microsoft SharePoint Team Services site or a Microsoft FrontPage Web site, from Microsoft Visual

SourceSafe, or from some other program that offers version control. If you leave without checking in your files, what happens to the rest of your team? What if you win the lottery and never come back to work? What if you're hit by a truck and never come back to work? What if your computer crashes and all the work you did after you last checked out the file is lost and your boss decides—for you—that you're never coming back?

Don't be so selfish. Do yourself, your team, and your work a favor: make sure that you check in your files before you check out.

## Checklist Item #5: Reassign Outstanding Tasks and Projects

That is to say, pawn off your work on someone else. Yes, it seems sneaky at first, but hey, someone has to do the work or it just won't get done, right? Reports won't get sent out, the site will go stale, or your fleet of trucks will be stranded somewhere without a gas pump in sight. In other words, deadlines will go by, and I know you don't want to be the cause of all that suffering.

There are a couple of ways to do this to unsuspecting coworkers: you can reassign your Outlook tasks, or you can send e-mail messages with follow-up flags that will turn red while you're still on vacation. (Refer to the section "Organization: Start with Your Inbox," in Chapter 4, "Surviving Life in the Office," to review what flagging messages is all about.) Both of these are diabolical— that's what I like about them. But they are effective when it comes to making sure the work gets done. And that is what we're all here for, yes? My favorite way to do this is to reassign (pawn off) tasks that either I've assigned to myself or someone else has assigned to me.

### Be Respectful About Whom You Delegate To

Pawning off a project on a manager, an administrative assistant, or even a coworker can be tricky (if not downright invasive). It's a good idea to ask that person first, to see whether he's available to take on a certain portion of your responsibilities. It's also nice to imply that you will return that favor.

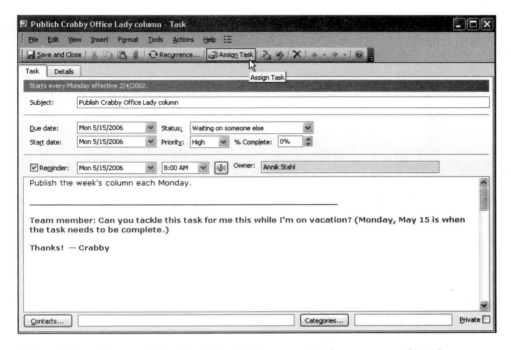

## Checklist Item #6: Decide What to Delegate and What Can Wait

Of course, how you handle delegation depends on what sort of work you do and how long you'll be gone. If you're an administrative or a personal assistant, or you have a job where you report to just one person, perhaps your boss can take care of certain duties herself, or if she is averse/allergic to that prospect, maybe you can ask another administrative assistant to help out. If you work as part of a team, you may need to do some delegating to a variety of other people. Managers, if they're worth their salt (and salary), should be able to help you with these decisions—but don't just toss it all on their shoulders. Being away can put a strain on your coworkers as well as your manager, so come up with a game plan that will spread the love around a bit.

# Checklist Item #7: Teach Your Inbox to Take Care of Itself While You're Gone

I use many rules in Outlook, and maybe you do, too. I have rules to move messages from one person into this folder, another person into that folder, and certain items get sent right to the Junk Mail folder. (Oh, how I love that rule like it was my child.)

Before you walk out the door, you may want to recheck how you've set up your rules and adjust them accordingly. For example, you may want to set up rules so that e-mail messages from certain customers are rerouted to the people you've pawned them off on instead of automatically having them shoveled into a deep Inbox folder that won't be touched until you return. You can do this from within the Out Of Office Assistant dialog box, or you can set up a specific rule.

**Note**  This checklist item is related to item #1 (setting your OOF). But instead of just letting your key customers know that you'll get back to them when you're good and ready, take advantage of the Rules feature in Outlook. That way, their messages can be sent to the people you've added as delegates for this particular account or project. (Setting up delegate information is described in Chapter 4, "Surviving Life in the Office.") The customers who need the most coddling won't feel lost, alone, and inclined to take their business elsewhere.

# Checklist Item #8: Notify Your Customers Up Front

This is related to item #7 (as well as the preceding note). Sure, you can notify your customers that you're not available with an out-of-office message. (And sure, they'll understand quickly when someone other than you responds to their e-mail.) But while I'm not a salesperson, that doesn't strike me as the kindest way to tell people that they'll be dealing with someone completely different now. Send your customers a note or an e-mail message or call them to let them know that you'll be gone for a while, and let them know whom they'll be working with in your company.

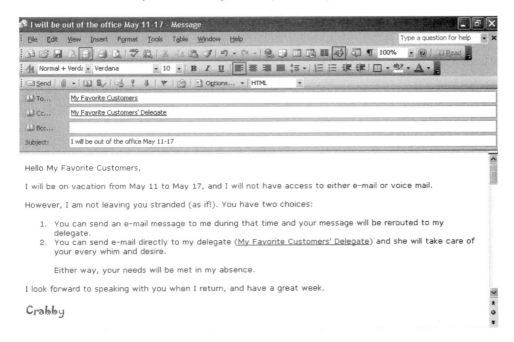

# Checklist Item #9: Get Your "House" in Order

"House" is in quotation marks because when I say *house*, I mean your house at work.

If you're a Type A personality, there's nothing like the feeling you get when you're checking items off a to-do list. If you're not a Type A, perhaps you have never experienced that feeling or are maybe even muttering to yourself, "List? What list?"

Either way, whatever "type" you are, you're now the type who's going to take a leave—extended or otherwise—from work, so consider putting yourself into high gear to wrap up whatever projects, tasks, or to-do items you still have hanging around. If you don't, and you haven't delegated them to anyone, they'll just be waiting there for you when you return. And like the fruit and dairy products in the fridge that you forgot to toss out before going on vacation, they may have bloated, created fuzzy green friends, or gone stale by the time you return.

# While You're Gone

Good for you—you've taken the preceding steps to ensure that you won't return to an out-of-control Inbox, overdue projects, resentful coworkers, or all of the above. Now that we've covered some of the items that you need to check off *before* you leave, consider how you want to handle communications while you are *in absentia*.

Depending on the policies of your company as well as your role within that organization, you need to decide whether you're going to have any communication with work at all while you're away. In some instances, you might not have a choice: once you're on leave, you're gone, and they don't want to hear from you. However, there might be circumstances when you'll be required to check in periodically.

## When You're a Small Business Owner

Chances are, if you own—and normally run—a small business, you won't be able to completely disconnect. If I were you (and you know I'm not, since I neither own nor do I run Microsoft, and it certainly isn't a small business), I'd set up some ground rules with your employees (not to mention yourself).

Maybe you'll decide to check mail once a week, or maybe you'll have all or part of your mail forwarded to a separate, personal account. However you want to work it, remember that you're on leave for a reason; if you're logged on every day and just doing the work you'd normally do, that's called telecommuting, and that's a completely different activity (see Chapter 7, "Working It from Home: Tips for Telecommuters").

# Welcome Back: Preparing for Your Return

OK, now you're back and about to jump into the fray again. It might be a bit of a struggle to figure out just where to start and how to get into that drone frame of mind again. And while I have some tips to offer, I don't have a one-size-fits-all solution or template to make this transition easier on you. I recognize that each person and each job is different, so consider these tips to be broad, and then take 'em or leave 'em.

**Don't expect to pick up right where you left off.**  You've just returned from spending two weeks in the sun, slugging mai tais as if they were about to become a banned substance. Or you've been dealing with a new baby, a sick parent, a sick self, or perhaps a personal issue or catastrophe. So take it easy on yourself, Sparky. Most managers and coworkers won't expect you to be at the top of your game right away. Try to not embrace all the stress you left behind right away. Give yourself some time to catch up on what's been going on. Talk to people, talk to your customers, read past issues of the company newsletters, and perhaps schedule some time for you and your manager to sit down and have a one-on-one.

**Let your coworkers know you're back.**  While this point seems obvious, and at the risk of sounding harsh (who, me?), life in the office has marched on without you, and it's possible that your coworkers have gotten along just fine in your absence. And while this is a good thing for business, it might make you feel left out. Stop by your coworkers' offices, send out a broad e-mail message, or gather the people with whom you work most closely in a meeting to try to catch up on what's been going on in your sector of the business.

**Decide when to turn off your out-of-office message.**  This point might seem to contradict the preceding one (about letting everyone know you're back), but it really doesn't. This is about, yes, letting people know that you've returned, but doing it in your own good time.

I know, it's weird to get an out-of-office message from someone who's been gone but whom you just saw in the lunchroom, and you may be the type to let those returnees know that their OOF is still on and to get with it. They're back and they're ready to open the floodgates and let the e-mail, meeting requests, and assigned tasks pour in, right? So some people, when they get back from their vacation or leave of absence, turn off their OOF right away. And yes, that is one way to tell folks you're back and ready to work.

However, consider handling this a little differently: instead of turning off the auto-reply you set up before you left, keep it on for a bit (a *bit*—a short time) but *change* the wording of your message to say that you've just returned from your vacation or leave and will get back to the sender shortly. You can still respond to the messages and meeting requests that start to gush in the moment your coworkers catch a glimpse of you. But people can be a lot more understanding than we give them credit for, especially if your message lets them know that yes, you're back, but still working on getting back into the swing of things. They won't feel ignored, and you won't feel overwhelmed.

# Getting Out of Dodge (Checklist Item #10)

You might be wondering why this item appears at the end of this chapter and not in the middle with the rest of the checklist items. Why? Because I don't want to end this chapter with you coming back to the office, fretting about what you missed while you were gone. I want you to be thinking about how great it is to really get away for a while.

OK, so you've set your OOF, you've marked off your calendar, you've reassigned tasks, and you've delegated to your heart's content. There are just a few more things you need to consider.

One more Ben Franklin quote: "Drive thy business or it will drive thee." While I agree that keeping up with work is well and good (not to mention necessary), so is planning for time away from work—or your drive for success may suffer.

- Don't leave your cell phone number on your whiteboard (unless, of course, you're prepared to receive frantic calls from a time zone 8 hours behind you).
- Change your outgoing voice mail message.
- Turn off your computer.
- Check the oil in the car.
- Make sure that your airline hasn't gone out of business.
- Take your nail clippers and knitting needles out of your carry-on bag.
- Turn off the lights.
- Don't forget to write.

Chapter Nine

# Ergonomics and Accessibility: Making It Easier on Yourself (and Others)

*Give me where to stand, and I will move the earth.*

*— Archimedes*

I've decided to combine two related issues into one chapter because, well, they *are* related. Without getting too up-close and personal here, both ergonomics and accessibility have to do with your body. You know, that body that you've had your whole life, the one that's seen you through the good times, the bad times, the injuries, and the growth spurts. The body you've possibly (hopefully) worked on to keep you healthy, to keep you looking good...and in the case of this chapter, to keep you effective and energized at work.

# Ergonomics and Accessibility: Cousins at Work

*Ergonomics* is about setting up your work area and your body so that you're comfortable and healthy while you're at work. Put simply, it's a means of figuring out a more comfortable way to do your job, whether you're a desk jockey, a grocery store clerk, a truck driver, a doctor, or a mechanic. Incorporating ergonomics into your daily work life makes you a more efficient and productive worker (which in turn, has the ability to make you a happier person in general).

## The Mind/Body Connection: Not Just a Pop-Culture Fad

If you don't make your workspace a place where your mind and your body can work together to achieve their potential, and if you don't take advantage of what you can do with Microsoft Office and Microsoft Windows technologies to make the programs do what you need them to do, you're letting your body and your mind (and frankly, me) down.

Now, as for what accessibility is and how it might relate to what you do, consider the idea that everyone sees, hears, feels, and maneuvers around the world differently. Accessibility means making something usable to everyone—including people with disabilities. That's why accessibility features—technologies that accommodate those of us with less than perfect vision, hearing, or dexterity—encourage everyone to get the most out of Microsoft Office (and computing in general). Are you seeing how these two ideas are related? They're both about getting the most out of your workday, no matter who you are, what you do, or how you want to do it.

In this chapter, I'm going to cover what ergonomics is and how you can apply it to your work life. I'm also going to show you some of the ways to take advantage of the accessibility features built in to Office programs so that you can make the most of them. After that, we'll look at how to make (and use) the documents, spreadsheets, presentations (and whatever else you're creating with Office) more accessible for everyone—including yourself.

In other words, this chapter is about making the tools you have work for you, and also about avoiding discrimination, as unintentional as it might be.

# Ergonomics: Healthy People Are Productive People

You know that you feel better when your body is in good shape, so why do you let your intentions fall to pieces the minute you step through your office door? It's time to think about staying in shape while you're at work, too. (And no, this doesn't mean taking two hours to go to the gym in the middle of the workday,)

Here's a personal example of what I mean. Recently, I bought a new bike. My 10-year-old mountain bike had become too much for me to bear; it hurt my rear end, my shoulders, and my back. And dragging my 4-year-old daughter behind me in a trailer didn't help matters.

When I first bought this expensive contraption, it had all the latest bells (literally) and whistles (not literally) that money could buy at the time. But time has marched on...and so has my body—it's just not the same body it was 10 years ago. (Frankly, it's not even the same body it was 3 years ago. Being in that over-40 age group has its advantages, but the "time-marching-on" feature is not one of them.) And yet I waited, oh, 6 or 7 years to buy a new bike. And why is that? Because I'd gotten used to the pain, the irritation, and the sore buns, that's why. And it didn't occur to me that bicycle technology had improved—markedly so—over the years.

But after a trip to my neighborhood bike shop, I tried a new kind of bike, one that suited my body, my lifestyle, and me better. And wow, what a difference it made. Now that I have my new bike, I'm kicking myself for not getting it sooner because now I can ride longer, have more fun, and cause little stress to my body. Makes sense, doesn't it?

Now, apply this to your own life: You make sure that you spend time at the gym, take the stairs instead of the elevator, and even drag yourself out of bed to greet that child of the morning—Homer's "rosy-fingered Dawn"—to jog through the cold morning streets so that your body stays healthy. (In case I lost you, that's Homer the classical Greek poet, not Homer the bald nuclear power plant employee.) But when you show up at work, does your back begin its daily slump? Do your shoulders start talking to your ears? Does your wrist start to twitch at the sight of that cute and (at first glance) apparently harmless little contraption called the mouse? If so, it's time to make some changes (because now you're starting to resemble that other Homer).

## What Is Ergonomics (and Why Should You Care)?

*Ergonomics* is literally "the study of human work." (In Greek, *ergos* means "work" and *nomos* means "of the natural laws.") For some of you, that might sound about as fun as watching paint dry. But you'd be wise to pay attention to this word, as it can affect your work and your health, As I alluded to earlier in this chapter, finding a way to make your workspace comfortable (for all professions and for all parts of your body) can only serve to make you more productive (not to mention happier) at work.

Luckily for us, some folks have made the study of ergonomics their life's work, and that's a good thing—they're helping the rest of us stay healthy, happy, and productive at work. In fact, at Microsoft, we have a whole team of ergonomics consultants that makes house calls. This means that if you work here, at your request, one of these people will come to your office, observe your style of working (the physical layout of your desk, chair, workstation, and so on), and then make suggestions about how to make you more comfortable and efficient.

And while your company might not have a specialized ergonomics team (or perhaps you work at home), many resources are available to help you on your way to becoming a more comfortable, more efficient, and healthier worker bee.

Start with the U.S. Department of Labor Occupational Safety & Health Administration's (OSHA) ergonomics Web site, at www.osha.gov/SLTC/ergonomics/index.html.

# Applying What Crabby Learned to Your Own Work Life

But no, I'm not going to just send you off to a governmental Web site (which, if it's anything like the Internal Revenue Service's Web site, will march you around in circles...that probably isn't good for your posture, anyway). I want to give you some basic tips that I garnered from my own experience with one of our ergonomics consultants. I swear, her visit was akin to having a personal trainer step into my office, right when I needed her the most. I was amazed at how the small changes she encouraged me to make affected my comfort level while at work—and you will be, too. As I learned very quickly (and still manage to put to use today), small improvements to your work environment can result in immediate improvements in your comfort levels. (Instant gratification, huh? Sounds OK so far.)

**Note** The following tips are for people who use computers to accomplish most of their work. However, all kinds of guidelines exist for all kinds of industries, from nursing to poultry processing. You can find information about all this on the OSHA Web site mentioned earlier.

## The Neutral Posture

If you practice Pilates or yoga, you already know what this is. *Neutral posture* refers to the resting position of each joint—that is, the position in which there is the least amount of tension or pressure on nerves, tendons, muscles, and bones. It's also the position in which muscles are at their resting length, neither contracted nor stretched. (This is where Pilates, yoga, and ergonomics part company. When you're practicing Pilates or yoga, you start in neutral posture, yes, but then the exercises and poses that you move into from neutral posture are all about contracting, stretching—and sometimes even contorting.) Here's how your body should be:

- Your lovely fingers are gently curved, in their natural resting position. They're not spread apart, and they're neither fully straightened out nor tightly curled. (For goodness sake, relax! Typing with balled fists makes for lots of errors.)

- Your wrist is in line with your forearm. It's neither bent up nor bent down, and it's definitely not bent toward the thumb or toward the little finger. (Ouchie!)

- Your shoulders are in a resting position, not pulled forward, back, down, or elevated. (They're calm, at peace, and lying in the sun on a beach.)

- Your head is balanced atop your spinal column. It's not tilted forward, back, or to either side, and it's not rotated to the left or right. Look straight ahead, kid. (If you're the vain type, place your mirror, well...ditch the mirror.)

## Be Comfy at Your Computer

You probably spend as much time with your computer as you do with...your pillow. And of course, you know what kind of pillow you like. Me, I like a big, fluffy, down-filled pillow (the more feathers, the better). My best friend travels everywhere with her flat (and frankly, almost paper-thin) pillow. And my daughter, well, she doesn't care what type of pillow she has, as long as the pillowcase is pink.

But when it comes to ensuring that your body is comfortable and able to perform at its best when you're in front of your computer, there are a few basic rules that everyone should consider incorporating. It's not a matter of size, hardness, thread count, or color at this point. Ergonomics experts have done many studies to try to determine the chair, workstation, monitor, and lighting situations that work best for most people. (In this case, one size *does* fit most.)

**Adjust your chair.**    You want to make sure that your thighs are parallel to the floor, with your knees bent at about 90 degrees. Your feet should be supported by the floor or a footrest. Because your body weight rests on your spine (if you are not spineless, which we assume you are not), your backrest should be positioned to support your lower back while you're typing and mousing.

**Adjust your workstation.**    Your work surface should be approximately one inch below your extended fingers when your elbows are at right angles to your sides. (I know this may seem a bit low, but trust me—it works.) Your keyboard and pointing device are within reach when your elbows are at right angles to your sides. Any materials and/or devices that you use frequently are within easy reach.

There is a variety of adjustable and ergonomic keyboards—some with curved key beds, others with padded palm rests—designed to help you keep your elbows, wrists, and fingers working together happily.

**Adjust your monitor and lighting.**    The top third of the viewable screen should be in line with your eyes when your neck, shoulders, and back are in neutral position, or a bit lower if you wear graduated lenses. You should also be able to read text and graphics easily at a distance of 16 to 28 inches.

## Step Away from the Computer

As I mentioned earlier in this chapter, you probably spend at least a bit of time trying to make sure that your body is (or is on its way to becoming) healthy. When you plop yourself down in front of your computer, all that energy and awareness need not just go by the wayside. There are a few easy things that you can do to ensure that your body, the one that carries you around all day, stays happy and healthy even while you're at work.

**Get up.**    Take a walk outside, through the halls, or even in circles around your office or cubicle—just get up and move occasionally. Every couple of hours, think of your computer screen as Medusa (that serpent-haired monster of Greek mythology): you will turn to stone if you don't take a break and look away.

**Stretch.**    When you're exercising, you know how important it is to stretch before and after your workout. When you're at your desk, it's just as important, and you should stretch often, not just at 8 and at 5. Stretch your neck; your hands, wrists, and fingers; your arms, shoulders, and upper back. And don't forget your chest: breathe, baby; breathe.

## For You Laptop Jockeys

Laptop users are everywhere, thanks to the preponderance of *hot spots* (high-speed wireless Internet access in public locations). Watch these laptop jockeys and you might see a majority of them hunched over, their fingers at odd angles to their keyboards, their shoulders up near their ears. If this is you (or if you're afraid it might become you), take some steps to make sure that your mobile workstation is as ergonomically correct as your stationary one.

In other words, stick with the neutral posture idea. Just because you're not at your desk, don't let this posture go to you-know-where in a hand basket, or your relaxing time in a café with your work might end up causing you more pain than it's worth.

## Employees: Ignore the Warnings and Risk Your Health

So, now you know a little about ergonomics. And if you choose to laugh off my warnings? Let's see...

You could incur a work-related musculoskeletal disorder (MSD). MSDs are injuries that can result from repeated strains or overuse and are sometimes referred to as cumulative trauma disorders, repetitive strain injuries, and repetitive motion injuries, among other terms. (Sounds like a real good time, doesn't it? Sick leave, not being able to pick up your toddler, walking around with splints and Ace bandages, and otherwise advertising your inability to care for your body at work...)

I'm sure you've heard of some of the following MSDs before:

- Writer's cramp
- Tennis elbow
- Pitcher's arm
- Milkmaid's hands (an oldie but a goodie)

Yes, that's right folks; don't you just love to think about the sprains, strains, inflammation, degeneration, pinching, and tears (the ripping kind and the crying kind)? How about shooting pain, fatigue, and numbness and tingling in your hands or feet?

All of that sounds like fun, doesn't it? Of course, repetitive strain injuries appeared a long time before ergonomics was a common term, and people sucked it up and thought it went with the job. But now we know more about soft tissue injury. So you (and your employer) have no excuse! And speaking of employers...

## Employers: Ignore the Warnings and Risk Your Workforce

Company owners, managers, and even CFOs: it behooves you to put an ergonomics plan into effect for your employees.

It's worth the cost to accommodate your worker rather than pay for medical care, training, and retraining, as well as other expenses incurred when an employee is injured on the job. And note that some states already have ergonomics laws or guidelines in place to encourage employers to be proactive in preventing injuries from occurring.

## Calculating the Employer-Related Costs of Strain-Related Injuries

Recent studies have found that in any given year, repetitive strain injuries represent about 62 percent of all North American workers' compensation claims and result in $15 billion to $20 billion in lost work time and medical claims each year.

In addition, a Microsoft survey found that 50 percent of study participants reported repetitive strain symptoms during the first year of their new job, and 68 percent of actual reported symptoms were deemed to be severe enough to be classified as a musculoskeletal disorder.

Consider those numbers when wondering whether a dedicated ergonomics team might be a good choice for your company.

In other words, as you, a fine, upstanding, and caring employer already know, it's less expensive to be proactive in preventing your employees' injuries than reactive in accommodating employees after they've been injured on the job by something that could have been prevented. As self-serving as this may sound, I'm happy to work for a company that expends the needed time, energy, and money to ensure that its employees have access to a highly trained ergonomics team.

Back to you employees for a moment. If your employer isn't quite so "with it" in this regard, please take the time to educate yourself about how you can protect your own health and safety while you're at work. Maybe even consider approaching upper management about putting certain ergonomics standards into place. Someone has to hoe that first row, right? It could be you. (I am, as you might guess, all about hoeing first rows and totally support you in this endeavor.)

# Accessibility Features Make All of Us Less Crabby

Now that we've covered some of the ways to make your workspace actually *work* for you without physical strain, what about making your documents, Web pages, presentations, and other Office files useful—not to mention comfortable—for both you and the people for whom you're writing? This is where accessibility comes in.

A little statistic that might surprise you: according to the U.S. Census Bureau, more than 50 million people in this country have some sort of disability. Very few of us have 20/20 vision, perfect hearing, and 100 percent use of every single part of our bodies. In fact, among adult computer users in the United States, 1 in 4 has a vision difficulty, 1 in 4 has a dexterity difficulty, and 1 in 5 has a hearing difficulty. But even if you don't have any issues regarding vision, dexterity, or hearing, chances are you know, work with, or love someone who does. And as the computer-using population grows older, these numbers are bound to increase.

For a more in-depth look at what accessibility is and how it affects millions of computer users, read "Understanding Accessibility," at go.microsoft.com/fwlink/?LinkId=62961.

Software, document, and Web site designers—if they're worth their salt, and their salary—design their products with all of this mind. In other words, we're all in this together, folks.

At Microsoft (and hopefully, at other companies that make computing software and hardware), people are striving to build technology that everyone can use, including those with physical difficulties or disabilities. I'm here to point you toward some resources that will help you get the most out of your software so that you can get the most out of your computer time and then get on with your day.

## What Is Accessibility Exactly?

As you've seen in this chapter and elsewhere in this book, *accessibility* refers to features in Microsoft Office (and in Microsoft Windows, too) that make things easier to see on screen and easier to access with the mouse and keyboard.

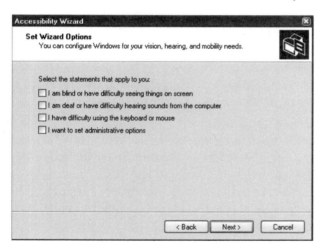

This could mean software makers making programs more accessible to the consumer, or it could mean you—those of you using the software to create your own applications—being given the ability to make your documents, presentations, and Web pages more accessible to your customers, your coworkers, and yourself. And how do we all do this? Read on.

# Using the Specific Accessibility Features in Office

Some of the accessibility features in the various Office programs overlap (for example, certain keyboard shortcuts), and some are specific to the individual applications. For example, in Microsoft Office Access, you can use the keyboard to define relationships, add or copy text boxes or other controls on forms and reports, and rearrange columns in Datasheet view. In Microsoft Office FrontPage 2003, you can run the accessibility checker to make sure that your Web pages are up to snuff.

Some of the features listed here (such as the ability to build accessible forms and the reading layout in Word) are Office-only accessibility features, and some are brought to you by our good friends on the Microsoft Windows team:

**Learn your keyboard shortcuts.** Keyboard shortcuts are the meat and potatoes (or for you vegetarians, the veggie burgers and peanut butter) of accessibility features for any program, whether it's Windows or Word. Maybe you have difficulty using the mouse or wish that you weren't so dependent on it. Give your mouse (and your wrist) a break: learn how to work with the keyboard in Office and start accomplishing tasks more quickly and easily with simple keystrokes. Using keyboard shortcuts can help you complete some tasks faster and more easily. Many features and commands are available directly by pressing two or more keys simultaneously. Press F1 in the program you're working in, and then type **keyboard shortcuts** in the Search For box to get a list of the shortcuts available in that program. (Many of these shortcuts overlap from program to program, saving your brain space for more tender memories.) Take a free training course on how to work with keyboard shortcuts at go.microsoft.com/fwlink/?LinkId=64290.

**Automate tasks.** You can also reduce keystrokes in most Office programs by automating them with a macro. A macro is a series of commands and instructions that you perform one time, recording them as a single command, and then using that command—that *macro*—to accomplish the recorded task automatically. For example, you can create a macro in FrontPage to make new pages and apply templates to them. It's like having your own self-created robot doing your bidding. (Create a macro to clean my house and pick up after my dog, and you'll be my new best friend.) Read more about what macros are and how to automate tasks by using them at go.microsoft.com/fwlink/?LinkId=64291. (Although this article is about automating tasks in Outlook, it pertains to any sort of macro you want to create, in any Office program.)

**Choose high contrast for readability or use the Zoom feature.** You can choose a High Contrast color scheme to improve legibility. Read about how to do this at go.microsoft.com/fwlink/?LinkId=62963. In addition, in most Office programs, you can also zoom in on your files—using either the Zoom feature (click Zoom on the View menu) or certain types of mice—to make information more readable on the screen.

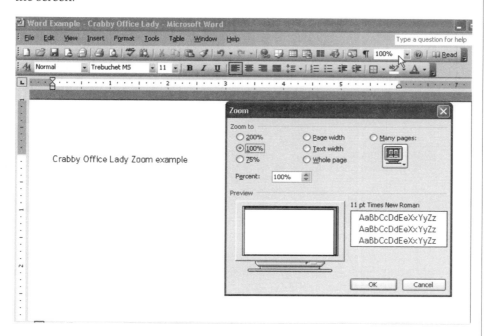

**Get a better view.** With Reading Layout view (introduced in Word 2003), if you're opening a document primarily to read it, the text is automatically displayed using Microsoft ClearType technology (if you're using a flat-panel monitor, a laptop computer, or a Pocket PC). These devices use LCDs (Liquid Crystal Displays), and ClearType makes the words on LCDs look almost as sharp and clear as if they were printed on a piece of paper. In addition, Reading Layout and Reviewing are the only toolbars that are displayed—all other toolbars are hidden, giving you more room for the document. Check out this demo about the Word reading layout view at go.microsoft.com/fwlink/?LinkId=62967.

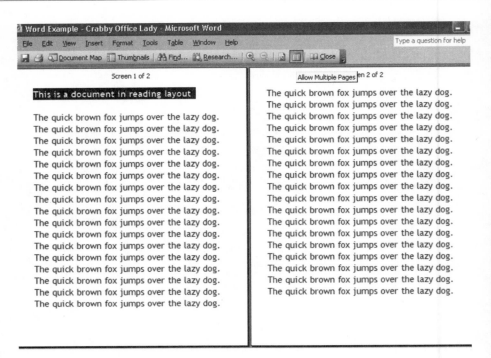

**Customize toolbars and menus.** You can customize toolbars and menu commands in most Office programs to put the most-used commands within easy reach. For more information, take the online training course "Customize Your Toolbars and Menus" at go.microsoft.com/fwlink/?LinkID=64289.

**Talk to your computer.** Speech recognition is installed in all Office programs by initially using the feature in Word 2003 or by performing a custom installation. Learn how to install and train speech recognition for all the Office programs that offer this feature at go.microsoft.com/fwlink/?LinkId=62965.

**Let your computer talk to you.** Narrator is a text-to-speech utility for people who are blind or have low vision. Narrator reads what is displayed on the screen—the contents of the active window, menu options, or text that has been typed. Read more about using Narrator at go.microsoft.com/fwlink/?LinkId=62964.

---

To read more about how to make your computer easier to see, hear, and use, visit the Accessibility site on the Microsoft Web site at go.microsoft.com/fwlink/?LinkId=62972.

---

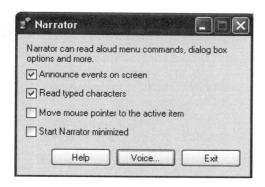

See? Perhaps you were under the impression that certain aspects or features of Office weren't available to you because of a limitation or particular disability you might have, but now you know that's not true. I'm here to tell you that in most cases, there are ways to work the way you want to work.

## Creating Accessible Office Documents

Now that you have the information you need to *use* Office documents, what happens when you're the one *creating* them? There are rules when it comes to creating the various types of documents, drawings, spreadsheets, and so on so that they're accessible to everyone. You want to make sure that your message isn't being lost because of the way you're sending it. Office offers a variety of ways to ensure that this doesn't happen.

**Create accessible Web sites.**    FrontPage enables you to create sites that are more accessible for people with disabilities. It also includes an accessibility checker to identify accessibility problems in your site. One of the most useful things this report does is to help you make sure that your links, images, and buttons are accessible to screen reader software. A screen reader verbalizes, or "speaks," anything on the screen, including all those links, images, and buttons that you've put on your Web page. Basically, it transforms a *graphical user interface* (GUI) into an *audio interface*, and it's essential for computer users who are blind or have limited vision.

**Build accessible forms.**    Microsoft InfoPath (introduced with Office 2003) is a great way to build and share forms, and its user interface supports most of the accessibility features in Windows XP.

**Create accessible Office documents.**    You can learn how to do this in Word, Visio, PowerPoint, Project, or any other Office program.

For specific information about, and procedures for creating, any type of accessible Office files, visit the Assistance Center on Office Online (go.microsoft.com/fwlink /?LinkId=59421), select the program that you're working in, and do a search for **accessibility**. You can also visit the Office Training home page (go.microsoft.com /fwlink/?LinkId=25327) and do a search for **accessibility** there. You'll find much more information in these two Web sites than I can fit into this chapter.

## Beyond Office

Office isn't the only product that tries to make your computer easier and more comfortable to use. Windows XP, Internet Explorer, and other Microsoft products also have built-in accessibility features.

But even going beyond Microsoft, there are many *assistive technology products* created by various manufacturers to provide additional accessibility to those individuals needing it. These include alternative input devices (such as touch screens and sip-and-puff systems, activated by inhaling or exhaling), Braille embossers, reading tools and learning disabilities programs, screen readers, and voice recognition products.

For more information about what's available and who the manufacturers are, visit the Assistive Technology Products Web site at go.microsoft.com/fwlink/?LinkId=62971.

## Pressing Onward with Assistive Technologies

And there you have it. Why should you, I, or anyone else who has some sort of impairment be restricted from the kind of software we want to use? We shouldn't be. Period. You're not the kind of person who gives up so quickly, and neither am I. Together we can figure this out and use some accessibility features to do it.

# The Family Reunion: Ergonomics and Accessibility

Now you should have a pretty good idea of how you can make your workspace and the programs you work with better suited not only to the way you work, but also to the way your body works. We all have our individual sensitivities, characteristics, and specific impairments that can hinder our progress at work. And while I know it might take some time to figure out how best to arrange your furniture, your elbows, your screen, and the programs you work with, I believe it's worth the effort, in the end, to take the time to do it. Think of this as an investment in your career and your health. Your body will thank you, your job performance will reflect your efforts, and you might just set a good example for those around you.

Taking some time to figure out how to make the most of your workspace and the tools you use will ensure that you have time and energy (not to mention health) for the future.

Chapter Ten

# Making the Most of Microsoft Office Online

*Help thy brother's boat across, and lo! Thine own has reached the shore.*

— *Hindu proverb*

Don't look a gift horse in the mouth. Forewarned is forearmed. Many hands make light work.

Wonder what I'm talking about? I'm talking about the tools that you—trying to get the most out of Microsoft Office, of course—have at your disposal on Microsoft Office Online, the Web site that hosts the Crabby Office Lady columns and that's your go-to source for all things Office.

In a nutshell (or if you're allergic to nuts, in a summary), this chapter is all about the different routes you can follow on the Office Online Web site to make you better at your job—it's as simple as that. And, as you should know by now, this is my goal as the Crabby Office Lady—my credo, if you will—and one that I take seriously to ensure that you have time for other things (such as, oh, I don't know, life outside the workplace).

## Office Online: Why Aren't You Already Intimately Familiar with It?

In case you haven't figured this out already, if it weren't for Office Online, Crabby would not exist—except in my own cranky heart. And frankly, I'd be a lot more acerbic than I already am if I didn't have access to all the information this site provides. (And, in turn, so would you.)

I want to come clean with you: I'm feeling somewhat slighted—if not insulted—by some of the e-mail messages and feedback I get from my column readers asking how to do *this* and how to do *that*, when just about everything they and you need to know, do, and accomplish is documented on the Office Online Web site.

If you're a regular reader of the Crabby Office Lady column (which, by the time you read this, will have been going strong—and gaining momentum—for at least five years), you know that I often refer to (not to mention *count on*) the assistance articles, templates, clip art, training, demos, quizzes, and every other type of content on the Office Online Web site. So what's stopping you from getting out there and exploring all that's available (not to mention *free*)?

Regarding the word *help*: we are all in need of it from time to time. (I mean *all* of us, so listen up, all you Lewis and Clark wannabes, there is no shame in asking for directions.)

Everyone learns differently. Some learners do really well when the teacher first explains a task verbally and then performs the task while the learner is watching. Other learners like to try to accomplish the task while watching the teacher do it at the same time. And still others prefer to jump right in there, allowing trial and error to guide their way.

So let's resume the beguine. (Remember what a *beguine* is? The ballroom dance, similar to the *rumba*, but with the accent on the second eighth note—you *have* been practicing, right?)

# Getting Real Help, Just the Kind You Need

I know you (because I *am* you): You're busily working in a program, be it Microsoft Office Word, Microsoft Office PowerPoint, or some other Office program. You've hit a snafu, whether it's a formatting frustration, a mail merge conundrum, or perhaps a complicated animation issue that's sucking up your time and eating away at your patience. In other words, you need help, and you need it *now*. So being the knowledgeable Office user that you are, you press F1 and perform a search using a (what you think is) logical term or phrase that describes what you're trying to do. Maybe you find the answer; maybe you don't. If you do, great—that's what we strive for. If you don't, your blood pressure rises, and your goodwill toward the tools you use starts to rapidly wilt.

## When You Write Directly to Crabby

I receive more than 1,000 e-mail messages and pieces of feedback (gathered from the site's database, which sends all your Crabby Office Lady column comments to me) each month. While I'd love to be able to help each and every one of you with your thorny problems and Microsoft Office conundrums, I just can't. It's not that I don't want to. In fact, so many of your messages are easily answered—but ah, there's the rub…

My goal (my *job* actually) is to write a weekly column (and now a book) that not only offers you *ideas* about how to work more productively and efficiently (thereby having more time for yourself, outside the office), but also *guides* you to the existing resources on the Office Online Web site (which, as you will discover, are aplenty). So please, before you pop off an e-mail message or a piece of finely crafted feedback to me, consider searching for what you need on this site. You are likely to find the answer (and find it a lot more quickly than if you had waited for an answer to come directly from me).

Unfortunately, some of you stop here and throw your hands in the air (and possibly your mouse against the wall) in frustration and despair. And then some of you write to me on the Web site to ask me how to solve your particular thorny issue, which I just can't do, considering the hundreds of inquiries I get each week. I wish I could help each and every one of you, but I just can't.

So….listen up, folks. I'm going to take you through the Office Online Web site, in case you're not already intimately familiar with all it has to offer you. Let's start at the most obvious: the Assistance Center.

## Assistance Articles

I'm not exactly sure how many good—not to mention ridiculously smart—people spend their days writing help topics and assistance articles for the Office Online Web site, but I know their offices encompass more than a couple of buildings on the main Microsoft campus in Redmond, Washington.

Just to give you a bit of background: every assistance article and help topic writer deals with a specific Office program, so you know you're getting information from an expert. The Outlook people are experts in all things Outlook; the PowerPoint folks know all there is to know about PowerPoint. In other words, you can trust what they write to be true (not to mention tested).

All of these writers of assistance articles and help topics are aware that we live in a bit of a vacuum here at Microsoft. Here's what I mean: we, as your go-to assistance writers, work on and use these programs all day, every day, and sometimes it's a bit of a challenge to figure out why you, our customers, can't understand how to use a particular feature or even a whole program. That's why we count on your giving us feedback about whether the article you just read was useful. We can then make adjustments to make that article better and more useful. But I'll get to how and when to give us feedback later in this chapter.

When you go to the Office Online Web site, you can go straight to the Assistance Center (go.microsoft.com/fwlink/?LinkId=59421) and then choose the program with which you need help. Or, on the Office Online home page, you can click the name of one of the programs that you need help with and then be ferried away to an all-encompassing program page that will give you not only assistance articles, but also things like product information, available downloads, and other information specific to that program.

For example, from the Microsoft Office FrontPage home page (go.microsoft.com /fwlink/?LinkId=63574), you'll be able to access training courses and demos specific to FrontPage, read columns by FrontPage experts, and also get a look at galleries of FrontPage customer sites.

FRONTPAGE HIGHLIGHTS

**Training and demos**

- Roadmap to mastering FrontPage 2003
- Get up and running with your first Web site
- HTML Tables I: Basic concepts
- HTML Tables II: Table and cell widths
- HTML Tables III: Design a page with layout tables
- HTML Tables IV: Format and touch up a page layout
- Demo: Code in half the time with new Split view
- More coding skills you should know

**Columns by FrontPage experts**

- Planning your Web site's information architecture
- Using color effectively
- Create dynamic ScreenTips
- So many browsers, so little time
- Create a dynamic school staff calendar with FrontPage 2002
- Subscribe to the free FrontPage newsletter

More...

**Gallery of FrontPage customer sites**

- The PR Guy
- Dougherty County School System
- Flathead County Search and Rescue
- Proudfoot Communications
- Rancho Fino

More...

As you can see, a visit to the Assistance Center (and the specific program home pages) is a great way to start trying to solve your problem. And even if you don't have a particular problem, you can learn new skills and get ideas about how to use each program more effectively.

# Free Online Training Courses

Let's talk about training. Again, some of us learn by reading, some by watching, some by doing. How about a way to take advantage of all three styles of learning? With a free Office Online training course, that's exactly what you get.

And that's why Office Online training has become so popular: it addresses many of your learning needs, no matter what those needs are. So no more whining that you're not getting the help you need, OK? It's all right there just waiting for you to explore. Now let's strap on our helmets, screw on those training wheels, and hit the streets.

Each week, the Office Online Training home page features a set of training courses highlighting courses that are "Built by Request," "What's Hot," or a "Featured Course"—one that the training team has chosen to feature and thinks might be beneficial to you.

The online training courses I'm talking about are not those multiday or multiweek courses that require you to take copious notes, send in assignments, or even prove to anyone (except, of course, yourself) that you've learned a darn thing. No, these are short courses—some of them with video and audio, and some of them with just audio—designed to teach you about a specific feature or task so that you can get on your way, finish up your work, and perhaps learn a new skill (thereby impressing your coworkers, your manager, and even your customers).

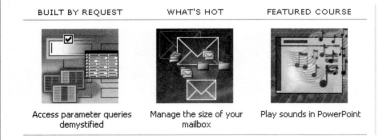

For more information about the huge variety of training courses available to you, visit the Office Online Training home page at go.microsoft.com/fwlink/?LinkId=25327.

# Demos

Office demos (short for *demonstrations*, not *demolitions*) are one of the most popular types of content on the Office Online Web site. And why not? When Microsoft began creating Office demos a few years ago, they were overwhelmingly positively received. It was as if you'd been waiting for these your whole life, and I can see why: they don't just tell you how to do something; they show you how and then link to other content that helps you get to work. And just like in Creative Writing 101 or Drawing 101, we all know that showing (rather than just telling) is a much more effective way to get the point across.

## Git Yer Red-Hot Demos!

When you visit the Office Demos Showcase page (go.microsoft.com/fwlink/?LinkId=50900), you can choose the demo you'd like to see from the lists of demos sorted by program.

Each demo offers different ways to access more content and information: some link to training courses related to the demo's main message; some give you the text, word-for-word, of what the demo says; and almost all offer See Also links that take you to assistance articles and templates related to the topic at hand.

## Types of Demos

If you're someone who likes to see the procedure performed before you jump right in there, Office demos are for you. They're not about learning by sitting in a straight-back wood chair with chewing gum stuck to the bottom of the seat. (In other words, demos don't offer the chalkboard, desks in rows, scary headmistress kind of learning.)

The demo gurus came up with a few types of demos to address your different learning styles.

**Step-by-step demos**     An example of a step-by-step demo is "Keep Column Names in Sight When You Scroll" (go.microsoft.com/fwlink/?LinkId=63579). In this demo, you learn that you can keep Microsoft Excel column names visible, no matter how far you scroll down the sheet, by freezing the names in place. This is one example of a demo that was created because of the frustration Office customers were having with this particular issue, and voilà, it's one of the most popular demos.

> ## Demo: Keep column names in sight when you scroll
>
> **Applies to**
> Microsoft Office Excel® 2003
>
> See all Office demos
>
>  Watch the demo ▶
> Isn't it frustrating when you lose sight of column names as you scroll down a worksheet? Scrolling up to the top to see the column names, and back down again for the data, you can start to feel like a yo-yo.
>
> But you can keep column names in sight, no matter how far you scroll down the sheet, by freezing the names in place. One click in your worksheet, and a click on a menu, that's all it takes. Want to see how?

**Demos that introduce new products or features**     Whether you're new to Office (Welcome! Where have you been?) or you've just installed a newer version of the program (Good for you! See—all that nagging about upgrading did pay off, finally!), often a demo is just what Doctor Crabby ordered—something to give you an up-close and personal look at some of the new or improved features that you don't quite "get"...yet. An example of this type of demo is one that reveals the Split view, available only in FrontPage 2003, "Cut Your Work in Half with the New Split View" (go.microsoft.com/fwlink/?LinkID=63565). After you watch this demo, you can refer to the text version of it if you missed anything or just want to review.

Keep in mind that a majority of the demos created by the demos team came straight from ideas that sent in by customers. Ask and ye shall receive.

**Demo: Cut your work in half with the new Split view**

**Watch the demo!**

Problems watching the video?
🛈 Try our troubleshooting tips.

Try Microsoft Office System Products

See all Office Demos

In Microsoft Office FrontPage® 2003, the new Split view gives you simultaneous complete control over both the design and the code of your Web pages.

In previous versions of FrontPage, you had to bounce back and forth between your design and code. Well, bounce no more. As you work with the design in Split view, you see the tags updated in the code. If you prefer to edit the code in Split view, one click shows your changes in the design. Save time. save work. This Split decision is a knock-out.

**Tour demos**    An example of a tour demo is "Learn to Use Clip Organizer" (go.microsoft.com/fwlink/?LinkID=63566). In case you're not familiar with the Clip Organizer, it's a handy program you can use to organize all the clip art, photographs, sound files, and animations scattered in your computer—content that you've downloaded from the Clip Art and Media site or even just other types of media files that you have stored on your computer. This demo shows you where Clip Organizer is, how to use it, and how to customize it for your own purposes.

**Demo: Learn to use Clip Organizer**

**Applies to**
Microsoft Office Clip Organizer

See all Office demos

Watch the demo ▶

Do you have a lot of clip art, photographs, sound files, and animations on your computer, but have difficulty finding what you want at the right time? You know they're somewhere, so why not organize them on your computer? Microsoft Office Clip Organizer is the tool for you.

Clip Organizer arranges and catalogs clip art and other media files stored on your hard disk. Learn how to make Clip Organizer work for you and quickly find the clips you need.

**Work Essentials demos**    Work Essentials, on Office Online, is the place to go to get advice and ideas from people working in your field, such as accountants, administrative assistants, or real estate agents (among others). The Work Essentials demos offer overviews of specific types of business practices, such as "Market Your Open Positions" (go.microsoft.com/fwlink/?LinkId=63567) for people working in human resources, and then usually point you to more information, such as templates and articles that you can use and read to find a particular solution.

Demo: Market your open positions

Watch the demo!

Problems watching the video?
Try our troubleshooting tips.

Try Microsoft Office System products
See all Office demos
See related tools for recruiting and employment specialists
Writing persuasive job descriptions that attract qualified candidates is essential in today's business environment. Learn how Microsoft Office Word 2003 can help you create compelling job descriptions and provide more enticing information to potential employees.

## Demos: Technical Details

Everyone has a different hardware setup and a different connection speed. Therefore, the demos might load quickly for one person and quite slowly for another. If you're having trouble accessing the demos themselves, be sure to click this link, found on every single demo page, for help: Problems Watching The Video? Try Our Troubleshooting Tips.

And don't forget, once the demo is playing, you can start, stop, and pause the demo. These controls might not be visible, so scroll down in the demo window to see them. Also, if the status is Ready, you'll need to click Play to start the demo.

You owe it to yourself to take a tour of the Office Demos Showcase to see what new Office features, programs, or Office Online products are waiting for you to discover them.

Visit the Office Demos Showcase at go.microsoft.com/fwlink/?LinkId=50900.

## Office Community

I'll admit it: sometimes I don't have all the answers. And I'll admit it for my cohorts too: sometimes Office Online assistance articles, help topics, training courses, and demos don't have the answers either. So what do you do when you desperately need an answer? Well, you have options.

- Blame me. (You laugh, but it happens.)
- Search for the answer on a Tibetan mountaintop. (Love those wireless connections.)

- Realize that others have had the exact same problem, and find out what they did to solve it. (Love that Office Community.)

Wait a minute—let's delve a bit deeper into that last option, the Office Community, which is sometimes referred to as a *newsgroup* or a *discussion group*. Whatever you want to call it, getting involved in an Office Community (whether it's the one that serves people using Word, Excel, FrontPage, or any other Office program) can be the best way to find an answer fast (and possibly make friends with a techno-smartypants). I mean, wouldn't you like to actually communicate with thousands of other people who are using the same products as you? And what about getting your answers from experts—such as Microsoft Most Valuable Professionals (MVPs)—for *free*?

---

**Note** No, there are no meetings, no dues, and no tearful confessions needed to become a part of the Office Community. But please, play nice and keep a cool head.

---

## Office Community Etiquette

Just like in team sports (and life in general), you'd be wise to learn and pay attention to the rules of the game when it comes to participating in Office Communities (or any online community, for that matter).

**Lurk before you leap.** You may feel a bit intimidated your first time out. Head on into a group, read some posts, do a search...and see what you come up with. Learn how people ask questions, and observe what kinds of questions garner the most useful answers.

**Search for existing answers before you ask.** If you have a problem with something, chances are someone has had the exact same issue, and someone more experienced than this person (or you) has come up with a solution. Before you start a new post, do a search and see what pops up.

**Be specific.** Create a subject line for your question that is concrete and focuses on the specific problem. Good subject: "Displaying contacts by last name in Outlook 2003." Bad subject: "Outlook irritates me."

**Don't hijack threads.** This means be relevant. If you've found a discussion thread about inserting and scaling graphics in a table in FrontPage, don't jump in there and start talking about graphics effects or how you can draw really great caricatures. Please stay on topic.

**Keep a cool head.** Please keep your posts sensible, clean, swear-word-free, and ALL CAPS–free. And if you feel angry enough to pop off an angry post, count to 10...and then go scream into your pillow. (Then rethink how involved you are in this software problem in the context of your life and try to put it into perspective.) Your engaging in *flaming* (the posting of obnoxious and rude messages) will just cause people grief—and possibly uncontrollable rage—and perhaps invite them to flame you back, igniting a flame war. There are enough wars going on in the world, Sparky.

**Limit the "Me, too!" responses.** It's a waste of time and discussion space to post a "Me, too!" response to a problem or answer. If you agree with someone's assessment of a problem, great. If you can expound on the subject or make the question clearer, even better.

**Do your part: vote.** Office Community offers a rating system for anyone who posts a message. Each time you read someone's post, you can rate it as helpful or not. This helps build the reputation of those who post useful information, and it can help you, as someone with a problem, figure out (pretty quickly) who gives good information.

---

To post a question (or even to answer one), visit the Office Community (also known as Discussion Groups) at go.microsoft.com/fwlink/?LinkId=63585.

---

As you can see, there are a variety of ways to access help when you need it. Pressing F1 (which opens the Help pane) is a great place to start, but it is by no means the only place to search for an answer to your problem.

# Making the Most of Your Office Documents

Sometimes a basic Word document just typed and printed out is all you need. But sometimes you need something a bit more, shall we say, exciting. Maybe you're preparing a PowerPoint presentation for a group of new employees and you want to spice it up with clip art. Or perhaps you want to make use of a template already created for a particular type of meeting, one that is happening in five minutes and that you just don't have the time to make all pretty and organized.

These are the times when specific areas of Office Online can come to your rescue.

## Templates

There are hundreds and hundreds of templates on the Office Online Template site, ranging from calendars and letterheads to student attendance records and greeting cards. The people on the templates team (and even some Microsoft customers) design these templates; you search for exactly what you want, download it, and away you go. You can use these templates exactly as they are, or more likely, you'll need to tweak them a bit.

My very first column was about how to customize templates. In fact, the idea to write this first column was born from some of the requests coming from Office customers, such as "I wish you would create a calendar template in Arial font in all red."

What the templates team at that time realized was that some customers didn't understand that the templates we provided on the site weren't set in stone—in other words, they were (and still are) meant to be customized. In this section, I'll guide you to the templates that are available, but I'll also encourage you to customize these templates to suit your needs.

Let's first take a moment to debunk three of the myths about templates.

## Myth #1: Templates Encourage Sloth

This one might be true if you just use a template exactly as it is and call it yours. I mean, how easy is that? Don't get me wrong: I already said that you *can* just use the available templates, add your content, and be done. But a little customization can go a long way. Let me explain.

Here in the online mailroom at Microsoft, we actually get e-mail messages from people requesting templates for movie scripts, and I don't mean just the blank pages arranged in a suitable way for writing content. No, I mean requests for screenplays, complete with story lines and fleshed-out characters. Can I assume that if we did post a real screenplay, one that one of our template creators spent five years of her life writing, it would be downloaded by some snip of a lad and passed off as his own? Will there be hundreds of the same scripts with the same characters and same plotlines being pitched to studio execs and then made into movies that are all (basically) the same?

(Wait. Been to the movies lately? Isn't that already happening?)

Rise above that! Do your own work! Show a little gumption and creativity! The key word here is *customize*, as in start with an existing template—a blank screenplay template, if you will—and then make it your own. (And anyway, who wants to produce a film about John and Cathy discussing styles and formatting in Microsoft Word?)

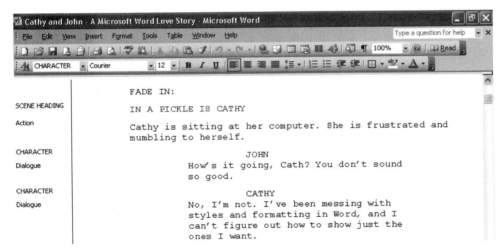

## Myth #2: You Can't Tell Anyone

Are you secretly downloading templates? Do you believe that downloading templates is something shameful? When someone compliments you on your document, do you feel a moral obligation to announce to the world that you created it from a template?

If you answered "yes" to any one of these questions, you need to snap out of it! What do you think we create these templates for, our health? It's OK to use templates, and it's OK to pass the work off as your own, providing you customize your templates. Repeat after me:

- I'm good enough.
- I'm smart enough.
- I'm creative enough.
- I just need a little help with customization.

## Myth #3: Smart People Don't Need Templates

Think of a template as an *idea* on which to expound. MSN Encarta Dictionary has this to say about it:

> *Template: something that serves as a master or pattern from which other similar things can be made.*

In other words, make someone else's good idea even better. Consider some of the world's inventors:

- **Henry Ford**

  **His claim to fame**: An automobile in every driveway.

  **His template:** The wheel and combustion engine.

■ **Mary Phelps Jacob**

**Her claim to fame**: A bra supporting every bosom.

**Her template**: A corset stiffened with (ouch) whalebone.

■ **Phil Donahue**

**His claim to fame**: A personality-driven talk show on every channel at every time of day or night.

**His template:** Public conversation and debate.

- **Howard Shultz**

  **His claim to fame:** A nonfat, half-decaf, half-regular, extra-hot, white chocolate caramel latte in every cup holder.

  **His template**: Italian espresso.

Get my point? Everyone has to start somewhere.

## Customization Puts You in the Driver's Seat

Now that I've set the record straight about the old wives' tales surrounding templates and you're all feeling better about yourselves, let's talk about practical ways you can make templates work for you. Whether you're working in Word, Excel, PowerPoint, or Access, customizing templates can become second nature to you after you learn a few tricks.

**Make Changes to Tables**   You template freeloaders—I mean, *downloaders*—seem to be a little hung up on tables. "There aren't enough rows," you moan. "There are too many columns," you complain. Good grief, get a handle on yourself! Here are some quick and easy ideas to make changes to a table (and no, these are not industry-insider secrets):

- Add a row, a column, or a cell.
- Add color to a table.
- Resize a table.
- Set border specifications.
- Merge adjacent cells (making one large cell).
- Split a cell (creating two or more cells divided into rows or columns).

**Customize the Font** So you don't like the choices the template creator made? You see yourself as much more jazzy, colorful, and sexy? Plain black Courier text just doesn't speak to you? Don't just sit there with your head in your hands; change the font!

- Change the font style, size, color, or effect. (Go crazy; change all four.)

- Use a different font family. (Courier irritates—not to mention bores—you? Maybe Verdana speaks to your inner artist.)

- Get crazy with WordArt. Express your deepest desires. (Uh, keep your audience in mind.)

**Customize Numbers, Dates, and Fields** When the Office Online Templates gurus sit down to create a template, they pretty much follow their own desires and tastes and do what they want with layout, design, and so on. While this is all well and good for their personal journeys, this doesn't help you. You feel hemmed in, restricted, and forced to adopt a way of thinking that you just don't subscribe to. (You think I don't understand restrictions? Have you any idea the type of edits this book and my columns go through?)

## What Does *Font* Mean?

*Font* basically means *typeface*. Examples of some of the more common computer fonts are Arial, Courier, and Times New Roman. A *font family* is a collection of all the *styles* (bold and italic are the most common styles) and sizes (10 point, 18 point, 48 point, and so on) of a particular font with the same typeface (such as Arial). The *font* is the starting point; what you decide to do with this font to make it stand out (bold, italic, underline, strikethrough, emboss, engrave, subscript, and so on) is your *font style*.

To put this in a real-world scenario, think of a wedding dress: it's usually white, it's usually flowing, it's almost always expensive. A Vera Wang wedding dress, however, has its own special style and its own particular flair—one that suits your particular needs and desires (and of course, bank account).

Hence, when you're picking and choosing fonts and font styles, select what suits your particular documents as well as your style. But don't forget your audience, either.

**Lists** If you don't like the numbering format or bullet styles that a list in a template uses, right-click the list and pick what you do like.

**Fields** Fields are used as placeholders for information that might change in a document. Say that the Word template you downloaded has a Date field inserted (which means that the date on the document is updated every time you open it). If you don't like the date format the template chose, you can change the format.

**Printing and page layout** Changing the way your document or spreadsheet looks on the page is easy enough. You can change any number of things, from the way the margins are set up to whether a multipage template prints double-sided.

Now see—that wasn't so bad, was it? And isn't your conscience starting to relax? (Good. Because my nurturing impulse has run its course.)

Using WordArt in your documents, presentations, and whatever type of Office file you're creating can create a fun, decorative effect. But use it sparingly; just like Outlook stationery, WordArt can detract from your message, which you don't want to do.

For more information about the various types of templates available to you (have I mentioned that they're free?), visit the Office Online Templates site at go.microsoft.com/fwlink/?LinkId=60514.

# Clip Art and Media

The Clip Art and Media site is, by far, the most popular area of Office Online. Folks are truly in love with adding clip art, photos, sounds, and even videos to their documents, presentations, and spreadsheets. And why not? With the huge selection this site offers, you're likely to find just what you need to make your documents sing. (But please, not too loudly or off key. Remember, a little goes a long way. You don't want your audience dazzled more by your art than by your message.)

From the Clip Art and Media site, you can download clips, copy and paste them, drag them into your documents, or even just have fun viewing them. And you can choose whether you want to see clip art (which is usually defined as collections of images, but in this case, I'm using it to include drawn images), photos, animations, sounds, or all of the above. Just type in a keyword and the type of clip you're looking for, and you're well on your way to spicing up those boring old documents. Or you can browse this very large collection by category, such as *abstract, nature,* or *technology*. If you're just not sure how to look or what to look *for*, view this demo for help: "How to Find the Perfect Clip Right Away" (go.microsoft.com/fwlink/?LinkId=63587).

Every piece of art used in this chapter (that isn't a screen capture taken from a program or something else on the Office Online Web site) was downloaded from the Clip Art and Media site on Office Online. Pretty fancy and fun, eh? (And notice: it's not overused.)

## Dazzle—Don't Destroy—with Clip Art

Just like overusing WordArt (or for that matter, funky fonts and stationery in e-mail messages), overindulging your documents with clip art will also muddle your message. While it's tempting to scatter your documents and presentations with photos, animations, and cute little smiley faces—particularly if you're new to Office—it can be distracting to your intended audience. Again, it's your message that counts.

## Getting Help While You're on the Clip Art and Media Site

To change how you see what the search engine—or browse feature—has come up with while you're on the Clip Art and Media site, click Options. You'll then have the choice to view the thumbnails (also known as *previews* of the clips) in a medium or a large size, and you can also specify how many images you want to see per page. Both these options are helpful, and I suggest you tweak them to suit your needs. For example, someone on a company intranet has more bandwidth for viewing images (no matter how large they are) than someone using a 56-KB modem (and so might choose to view more images per page).

**Clip Art and Media Options**                                             Help

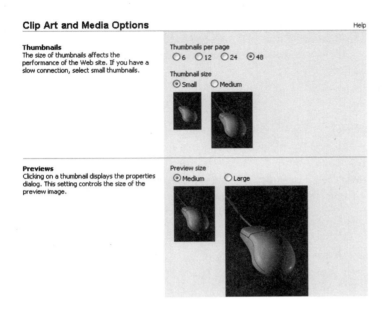

**Thumbnails**
The size of thumbnails affects the performance of the Web site. If you have a slow connection, select small thumbnails.

Thumbnails per page
○ 6   ○ 12   ○ 24   ⊙ 48

Thumbnail size
⊙ Small     ○ Medium

**Previews**
Clicking on a thumbnail displays the properties dialog. This setting controls the size of the preview image.

Preview size
⊙ Medium     ○ Large

---

For more information about getting the most of the Clip Art and Media site, refer to the demo "How to Find the Perfect Clip Right Away" at go.microsoft.com/fwlink /?LinkId=63586.

---

But that's not all—no, that's not all. (Can you tell that I hear Dr. Seuss in my head?) When you visit the Clip Art and Media site, you not only gain access to hundreds and hundreds of clips and photos (not to mention sounds and animations), you can also link to articles, templates, and training courses—resources that show you how you can incorporate those fabulous pieces of media into your documents, presentations, drawings, and more. The site not only leads you to water...it helps you drink.

---

**Caution**    I get many questions from my column readers asking whether they can use a clip for their newsletter, or their signature, or even their presentations. And the answer is yes...and no. The clips, photos, sounds, and animations available on this site are free for you to use, provided that you don't sell or distribute them, you don't change them to add *scandalous* or *naughty* words or images <tsk-tsk>, you include a copyright notice on any of the products that you sell that include Microsoft clip art, and last, you don't allow third parties to distribute copies of Microsoft clip art (except as part of your product or service). In other words, yes, you can use whatever you like to your heart's desire. But just be sensible, will you? Don't make us come and hunt you down for copyright violation. That just isn't fun...for anyone.

To take a look at what the Microsoft Office Clip Art and Media site has in the way of clip art, photos, sounds, and animations, visit go.microsoft.com/fwlink/?LinkId=9479.

# Office Marketplace

Office Marketplace is where you can try out, download, and purchase Office products and services or just get an idea of what's available to you as an Office customer. You'll find that different services do different things. For example, some are designed to enhance your snoozy PowerPoint presentations, while others help you manage your daily spam intake. It just depends on what you want to do and how you want to do it.

I like to think of Office Marketplace this way: There are some clothes in your closet that stand on their own (figuratively, I hope) in terms of functionality, style, and performance—for example, the little black dress. It's simple, classic, and appropriate for various types of functions.

But you may find that there are times when accessorizing will help you achieve more with your favorite ensemble. For example, add a pair of snazzy heels and a string of pearls to that simple dress, and you're ready for a night of fine dining. Or ditch the hose and add some strappy sandals, and you're ready for a sunny walk on a sultry beach. (Or is that a sultry walk on a sunny beach?)

You get my point: some things are great on their own, but everyone loves a little something extra or new. That's where Office Marketplace comes into play.

Office Marketplace offers hundreds of third-party tools for Office customers. So before you throw up your hands in despair because you think your program can't do something, check out what this site offers.

I'm not exactly sure how many Office Marketplace partners Microsoft has now, but I can tell you that there are a lot. And why do you think that is? Maybe because Microsoft Office is the most widely used productivity software in the business sector and other companies want to jump on that bandwagon? Could be. Maybe it's because Office programs have so many levels of functionality that people can be creative about how to add on to them to make them even more useful? It's possible. Or perhaps it's because these service providers just want to be part of the same Web site where Crabby's columns are. Again, could be. (But I doubt it—even I don't have an ego that big.)

You know how when you go to the mall, you're constantly trying to navigate yourself and your family through the gangs of teens (or "tweens")? If you look closely, you'll notice that one or two boys or girls in every group seem to be the leaders. Their hair is "better," their piercings more noticeable, and their clothes more fashionable. (To them, of course. I sure hope the whole "belly shirt" craze is over before my kid gets old enough to get wind of it.) But more important than their looks, they just seem to have an air of self-confidence and authority.

The same is true with Office Marketplace providers. Just like the leaders at the mall, no matter how many providers want to be on the site, not everyone makes the cut. Microsoft picks and chooses the best of the best to represent Office programs and the things they are capable of. These third-party software providers are leaders in their field' (and they didn't even have to show their belly to acquire that distinction).

OK, so now that you get the idea of what Office Marketplace has to offer, head on over there and take a look for yourself. In fact, many of the services on the site offer free trial periods, so you have nothing to lose.

For more information about what Office Marketplace and its participants can offer you, visit go.microsoft.com/fwlink/?LinkId=61381.

# Keeping Your Computer (and Your Fun Level) Up-to-Date With Downloads

If you want to keep up with the latest and greatest (not to mention the safest and most secure) downloads for any version of Office, there are two basic ways to do this: you can accomplish this automatically or you can do it manually, by visiting the Microsoft Office Downloads Web site or using the Help menu in any Microsoft Office program. It really just depends on what sort of download you need (security updates and service packs) and those fun extras you just want (add-ins, viewers, and so on).

Let's start with the automatic way—the means of keeping your computer up-to-date with critical downloads, without you having to think too much about it.

## Making Sure Your Computer Is Up to Date...Automatically

Microsoft highly recommends that you turn on Automatic Updates. When you do this, you can choose to automatically download and install updates as they become available, just download the updates and decide whether you want to install them, or just be notified when an update is available. You don't have to go to any Web site to try and figure out what you have or what you don't have; Microsoft Automatic Updates does it for you...automatically (good name for it, eh?)

**Note** To turn on Automatic Updates, click Start, right-click My Computer, then select Properties. Click the Automatic Updates tab and then make your choice.

Turning on Automatic Updates is a way to make sure that you're getting the latest Service Packs, security updates, and critical things like that.

## Making Sure Your Computer Is Up-to-Date...On Your Own Time

If you've decided to not turn on Automatic Updates (hey, I'm just here to suggest, not judge), you still need to check if your computer is up-to-date, and you can do this in a few ways:

- In any Office program, on the Help menu, click Check For Updates. This will take you to the Office Downloads page, where you'll click the Check For Updates button. When you do that, the Office Downloads program will scan your computer (and won't send any personally identifiable information to Microsoft, by the way) and let you know what you're missing. You can decide whether you want to download the list of updates you're shown. Office Update will indicate what is critical and what is just a suggestion.

- Go directly to Microsoft Office Downloads, and again, click that cute Check For Updates link. (It's near the top of page with a friendly green arrow in front of it).

- Order a service pack CD. Service packs tend to be fairly large, and if you're using a 56-KB modem, chances are you have neither the time nor the inclination to download a service pack. Thankfully, you can order a CD and have the service pack sent to you. Don't forget, though, that the postal person will need a few days to get that CD to your house.

For more information about how to order Office Service Packs on CD-ROM, visit go.microsoft.com/fwlink/?LinkID=63568.

No matter how you decide to install these critical updates regularly, pick a way that works best for you, and do it faithfully. Your computer will be less vulnerable no matter how you decide to do it.

# Getting the Add-Ins, the Converters, the Viewers...and Other Fun Stuff

Sometimes you just need a little something to tide you over until the next version of Office is released: an add-in, an update, or a white paper to wile away those long evening hours. Office downloads are here to help.

Think of a trip to the Microsoft Office Downloads Web site (go.microsoft.com/fwlink /?LinkId=8241) like a trip to the bank, the grocery store, or even the cosmetic surgeon: sometimes you just need to boost your financial power, stock up on necessities, or perhaps add a little fluff and well-being to your computing lifestyle. Office offers a variety of downloads designed to give you all of that and much, much more.

And here's the difference between a trip to Office Downloads and a trip to, say, the plastic surgeon: all of our downloads are free. That's right, *F-R-E-E*. As in complimentary, gratis, no charge. But on the other hand, as I view it, there are two parallels between plastic surgeries and Office downloads:

1. Certain cosmetic procedures (Botox injections, liposuctions, and chemical peels) and certain Office downloads (PowerPoint Viewer 2003, Office Sounds, and Outlook PST Backup) tend to be more popular than the other offerings among the general population.

2. Conversely, certain cosmetic procedures (such as chin implants) and certain Office downloads (such as the Microsoft Visual Keyboard add-in, where you can type in more than one language on the same computer) are often overlooked—you should perhaps explore these hidden gems more fully before passing judgment.

Visiting the Microsoft Office Downloads Web site not only allows you to pick and choose which downloads you need, but you'll also get a smattering of downright fun downloads that you never knew existed.

## Why So Many? Why So Often?

And finally, the ultimate question: Why does Microsoft have so many updates so often? In a word or two: we're all human, and we do make mistakes. But more than that, technology moves so fast that while we're busily fixing the issues that crop up after we make a product available, we're also coming up with newer and better ways of doing things. In other words, we come up with all sorts of neat-o add-ins and features that we don't have time to add to the regular main product. And frankly, we get many of our ideas for new features from you, the loyal customers. So why should we let a good thing get away?

If we waited until every download was perfect before making it available to you, all of our fun and useful downloads would be few and far between. You'd be waiting and waiting and waiting.

And so while we want to be competitive, we need to balance how long it takes to create the software with how perfect it is. We want to give you what you want since you're so discerning, but sometimes things don't go exactly as planned <gasp> or a security issue becomes known, and we need you to install an update. So if we ask you to update, please do. It's for your own good, dearie—we're not just trying to drive you crazy.

For more information about how to keep your Office products up-to-date, visit Office Updates FAQ at go.microsoft.com/fwlink/?LinkId=63577.

# Staying in Touch

We implore you to give us feedback about the various types of content on the Office Online Web site. But not all feedback is created equal. Here is some advice on how to send us comments that will hit their mark and make an impact.

Some of you already know about how to do this. In fact, some of you have offered insightful comments...and some of you have shaken your digital fists at me. See, I often get e-mail messages from my readers making suggestions about how to make a certain program or feature better. I also get comments about how the site search engine isn't doing the bidding of customers. And while I appreciate the time you take to write your well-crafted (though often crabby) messages, your efforts are, unfortunately, somewhat misguided. (Truthfully, comments like "You are all greedy pigs with no talent" don't really inspire us to do better and make your life easier.)

There are a few ways to offer feedback, give suggestions, and supply comments that will really get you somewhere.

## Talk to Us

Don't talk with your mouth full. Don't talk to strangers. Don't talk during the movie. Don't talk back.

Wait. While I think all those directives have value, that last one has no place on the Office Online Web site. We want you to talk back. We want your rants, your raves, your suggestions, and your thoughts on the matter. (And please, stick to the matter at hand, will you?)

When we can have communication between us, that is a good thing—a very good thing. What better way for you to let us know what is and isn't working for you? On Office Online, you can rate, in a variety of ways, all of the articles, columns, templates, training courses, demos, and Office Marketplace partners that are all part of this happy system of sites. You can also comment on a specific Web page, offer feature suggestions, and see what other Office customers are saying.

**Columns, articles, and tips**   You can let us know whether what you read was helpful, and you can tell us why or why not. Just look for the *Was This Information Helpful?* link at the bottom of each Web page.

**Training courses**   Each training course includes a Feedback link, which takes you to a page where you can rate the course itself and its level of difficulty. There is also room for your comments and suggestions. (And I can tell you that the training course team takes these suggestions very seriously. In fact, they often tweak existing courses and create new ones based on your feedback.)

**Office Marketplace listing**   Office Marketplace offers a *Rate This Listing* feature on each service description page, and you can also tell us why you rated the service this way. On that same page, you can see how others rated the service, too. If you want to become an Office Marketplace provider, or if you want to suggest a service, there's room to do that on the Office Marketplace home page.

## So I Talked—Now What?

I know what you're thinking: yes, I give my well-crafted feedback only to have it enter some netherworld within Microsoft. Well, you are quite wrong, my pessimistic friend.

When you give feedback about an assistance article, that feedback goes directly to the writer of that article! And the same for feedback about a template or a training course: your missive gets to the one person who can make a difference and save the world from the scourge of an awkward tip, an inappropriate graphic, or a badly constructed sentence. In other words, we're listening. So remember: If you can't say something nice, say something not nice. Just say it. But do consider saying it *constructively*. You can catch more flies with sugar than with vinegar (not that I've been known to subscribe to that notion, of course).

# The *Comment On This Web Page* Link

Now, if you want to tell us or talk to us about something a little more general—a specific home page that's gone awry with formatting or whatever—there is a way to do that, too.

On the various home pages within Office Online (*home pages* meaning the main Assistance page, the main Training page, and the various Office program main pages), you'll find a *Comment On This Web Page* link. Click the link, and you'll be whisked off to a feedback page that gives you plenty of room to offer your intelligent insight and witty remarks about the particular page you were on. Maybe you think the page is hard to navigate, maybe you think the content is stale, or perhaps you think the page changes too often. Whatever your thoughts, send them our way. You'll feel better, and if enough of you make a similar request, you might just find your idea implemented in living color on the site.

# The *Contact Us* Link

At the bottom of each Web page on the Office Online Web site is a *Contact Us* link that takes you to the Contact Us page (go.microsoft.com/fwlink/?LinkId=63575). Clicking that link takes you to a page with a variety of options.

**Contact A Support Professional**    Get personalized answers from Microsoft or other support providers. Note that some support options might incur additional costs. Which leads me to the next option...

**Get Answers From Other Office Users**    Here is one way to get *free* help. I use this option not only to get column ideas, but also to find answers to Office questions that I can't seem to figure out. Use the Ask A Question Wizard to search for answers in the Office Community. Most (if not *all*) of the questions you have are ones that other people have asked before. And not only do other Office customers answer questions, but our MVPs also spend a lot of time in the Office Community answering your burning questions. (And again, this option is always free.)

**Search The Knowledge Base**    Find articles on resolved customer problems and browse the current top issues.

**Report A Problem On This Web Site**    Report any broken links or unavailable pages here.

**Make A Suggestion**    Use the Make A Suggestion Wizard to submit ideas for any Office product or Office Online feature.

**Suggest New Content**    Have a template you'd like to see on the Templates home page? Not finding the type of clip art you so desperately need? Or perhaps you have an idea for a training course that you know many other Office customers could really use. Be proactive, and help Microsoft cast its assistance net even wider.

# I Know Which Side My Bread Is Buttered On

Office Online is the site I've referred to often in this book. I've incorporated procedures that have been meticulously tested (yes, by me, but first by those experts I referred to earlier) and documented on that site. I've also provided links to articles, demos, templates, downloads, and everything else that has to do with making you more efficient and productive (not to mention *happier*) in the workplace.

So as I wrap up this chapter (and this book), let me shout out a big thanks to the many people who make my work—and your Office life—useful. These people are the article, training course, and quiz writers; the template and demo creators; the site managers; the testers, program managers, and developers; and the design teams—all of whom spend long hours trying to ensure that you have the resources you need to make you more effective and, frankly, more adept at the work you do.

And now that I think of it, I need to add one more motto to the list I had at the beginning of this chapter: Don't bite the hand—the Office Online Web site hand, that is—that feeds you. And if our helping hand isn't feeding your Office needs, please, when you can, write us and let us know how we're doing. Someone reads every single piece of feedback that is sent to us about the various types of content on the Office Online Web site. We're here to help; it's what we're paid for. In other words, if you're not getting the help you need, we're not doing our jobs.

# Epilogue

*Humor is the only test of gravity, and gravity of humor; for a subject which will not bear raillery is suspicious, and a jest which will not bear serious examination is false wit.*

— *Aristotle*

And so we've made it through this book together. Maybe you're smiling; maybe you're guffawing; maybe you're scratching your head, wondering what in the heck this book was about and how on earth it got into print...

Well, no matter how you're feeling, you've reached the epilogue, and I thank you for the time you took in getting here. Now it's time for you to do a little work.

Remember, way back, in the introduction when I suggested to you that there might be a quiz at the end? Now that you're more enlightened about using Office and actually surviving life in an office, the time has come to prove your mettle. (Don't say I didn't warn you.)

# Are You a Crabby Office Person?

Before we jump into the real quiz, I want you to fill out my own personal questionnaire to help me determine whether you're a Crabby Office Person yourself. (Consider this a warm-up quiz.)

1. What's the first thing you do when you drag yourself into work every morning?
   a. Drop off the lattés and mochas that you brought for the whole gang.
   b. Turn on the coffee machine and let yesterday's grounds get a second soaking.
   c. Combine half-full cups on your desk and reheat.

   Answer: c

2. How do you respond to negative feedback from coworkers and managers?
   a. Look earnest and say, "I promise I'll try to work better and smarter."
   b. Look crestfallen and say, "I know I'm no good. I just needed someone to affirm that."
   c. Quote Marshall McLuhan: "A point of view can be a dangerous luxury when substituted for insight and understanding."

   Answer: c

3. When a group of subordinates is having an after-work whine session about management, how do you participate?
   a. Nod empathetically and say something positive about working well with others.
   b. Get some juicy gripes in there yourself.
   c. Spill your guts the next day to any manager you can find.
   d. Me? A subordinate? Yeah, right.

   Answer: d (No, not c. Even Crabby hates a squealer.)

So how do you know you're a Crabby Office Person? You chose the right answers, of course.

# The Real Quiz: How Well Did You Read This Book?

Now on to the real quiz. Take this short (and hopefully, fun) little test to see if you really did get the messages I was trying to convey in this book.

(Here's a hint: The answers are located somewhere in this book...)

**Question #1:**   Name three of Crabby's top 10 e-mail crabs.

**Question #2:**   What's the difference between a shortcut menu and a keyboard shortcut?

**Question #3:**   What feature makes it easy to insert long phrases or words without having to *actually type* them out time and time again? (Hint: It's the same feature that learns how to fix your typing mistakes, after you train it the first time.)

**Question #4:**   What's one of the three collaboration tools that you can use to avoid face-to-face contact with difficult coworkers?

**Question #5:**   What's one of the ways you can delegate part or all of a project to someone else?

**Question #6:**   What two ways can you prove to your manager that you're worthy of a raise or promotion come performance review time?

**Question #7:**   Name one telecommuting myth...and then refute that myth.

**Question #8:**   What are two things you can do at work—before you go on vacation—so that you don't come back to a load of work that will make you regret the time you spent away?

**Question #9:**   What's one way to improve your health and posture while sitting at your desk?

**Question #10:**   Name three ways you can get help from the Microsoft Office Online Web site.

If you enjoyed taking this quiz, proving to me (and yourself) that you paid attention for as long as it took to read this short little book, you'll probably enjoy the Office Online quizzes. They're one of the most popular types of content on the Office Online Web site. And why not? They're short, they're fun, and they can give your technical ego a boost.

## Take a Real Quiz and Test Your Skills

If you enjoyed taking the quiz at the end of this book, you will *love* the Office Online quizzes. There are quizzes about every single Microsoft Office program, including Picture Manager and Clip Art and Media, and even quizzes that cover Office basics. Taking a quiz is one of the best ways to evaluate where you stand when it comes to understanding—not to mention making the best use of—Microsoft Office. So take a quiz, check your answers, and if you didn't score 100 percent, you'll have the opportunity to learn more about why you missed the ones you did.

You can find all the Office Quizzes on the Office Online Web site at: go.microsoft.com/fwlink/?LinkId=61382.

Head on over to the Microsoft Office Quizzes Web site and test your skills, smartypants. And if you're not up to snuff, you can always read a Crabby column, take a look at an assistance article, take a training course, or... reread this book.

# Index

# Annik Stahl

With previous jobs ranging from journalist to deliverer of singing telegrams, and from espresso cart owner to Club Med employee, Annik Stahl believes she earned the right to create the character of the Crabby Office Lady. Therefore, in 2002, wanting to reach out to Microsoft Office customers in a more personal way, Annik created the grumpy but loveable character of Crabby. By fashioning this ultimate "power user," willing to share her expertise with a touch of humor, Crabby's (and Annik's) goal has always been to encourage her readers to enjoy their work more and become more efficient at it so that they can get up out of their chairs and get on with their lives. Annik lives in Denver with her daughter, Bian, who is (almost) never the Crabby Office Baby, and her Australian Shepherd dog, Ry (definitely never the Crabby Office Dog).

# Additional Resources for Business and Home Users

*Published and Forthcoming Titles from Microsoft Press*

### Beyond Bullet Points: Using Microsoft® PowerPoint® to Create Presentations That Inform, Motivate, and Inspire
Cliff Atkinson ● ISBN 0-7356-2052-0

Improve your presentations—and increase your impact—with 50 powerful, practical, and easy-to-apply techniques for Microsoft PowerPoint. With *Beyond Bullet Points*, you'll take your presentation skills to the next level—learning innovative ways to design and deliver your message. Organized into five sections, including Distill Your Ideas, Structure Your Story, Visualize Your Message, Create a Conversation, and Maintain Engagement—the book uses clear, concise language and just the right visuals to help you understand concepts and start getting better results.

### Take Back Your Life! Special Edition: Using Microsoft Outlook® to Get Organized and Stay Organized
Sally McGhee ● ISBN 0-7356-2215-9

Unrelenting e-mail. Conflicting commitments. Endless interruptions. In this book, productivity expert Sally McGhee shows you how to take control and reclaim something that you thought you'd lost forever—your work-life balance. Now you can benefit from Sally's popular and highly regarded corporate education programs, learning simple but powerful techniques for rebalancing your personal and professional commitments using the productivity features in Outlook. When you change your approach, you can change your results. So learn what thousands of Sally's clients worldwide have discovered about taking control of their everyday productivity—and start transforming your own life today!

### On Time! On Track! On Target! Managing Your Projects Successfully with Microsoft Project
Bonnie Biafore ● ISBN 0-7356-2256-6

This book focuses on the core skills you need to successfully manage any project, giving you a practical education in project management and how-to instruction for using Microsoft Office Project Professional 2003 and other Microsoft Office Professional Edition 2003 programs, such as Excel® 2003, Outlook 2003, and Word 2003. Learn the essentials of project management, including creating successful project plans, tracking and evaluating performance, and controlling project costs. Whether you're a beginner just learning how to manage projects or a project manager already working on a project, this book has something for you. Includes a companion CD with sample Project templates.

### Design to Sell: Using Microsoft Publisher to Inform, Motivate, and Persuade
Roger C. Parker ● ISBN 0-7356-2260-4

*Design to Sell* relates the basics of effective message creation and formatting to the specific capabilities built into Microsoft Publisher—the powerful page layout program found on hundreds of thousands of computers around the world. Many Microsoft Office users already have Publisher on their computers but don't use it because they don't think of themselves as writers or designers. Here is a one-stop guide to marketing that even those without big budgets or previous design or writing experience can use to create compelling, easy-to-read marketing materials. Each chapter has an interactive exercise as well as questions with answers on the author's Web site. Also on the Web site are downloadable worksheets and templates, book updates, more illustrations of the projects in the book, and additional before-and-after project makeovers.

### Microsoft Windows® XP Networking and Security Inside Out: Also Covers Windows 2000
Ed Bott and Carl Siechert ● ISBN 0-7356-2042-3

Configure and manage your PC network—and help combat privacy and security threats—from the inside out! Written by the authors of the immensely popular *Microsoft Windows XP Inside Out*, this book packs hundreds of timesaving solutions, troubleshooting tips, and work-arounds for networking and security topics—all in concise, fast-answer format.

Dig into the tools and techniques for configuring workgroup, domain, Internet, and remote networking, and all the network components and features in between. Get the answers you need to use Windows XP Service Pack 2 and other tools, tactics, and features to help defend your personal computer and network against spyware, pop-up ads, viruses, hackers, spam, denial-of-service attacks, and other threats. Learn how to help secure your Virtual Private Networks (VPNs), remote access, and wireless networking services, and take ultimate control with advanced solutions such as file encryption, port blocking, IPSec, group policies, and tamper-proofing tactics for the registry. Get up to date on hot topics such as peer-to-peer networks, public wireless access points, smart cards, handheld computers, wireless LANs, and more. Plus, the CD includes bonus resources that make it easy for you to share your new security and networking expertise with your colleagues, friends, and family.

---

*For more information about Microsoft Press® books and other learning products,*
*visit:* **www.microsoft.com/mspress** *and* **www.microsoft.com/learning**